# LAUGHING
# AT
# GROWING OLD

JOHN H. HACKER

I-FORM INK PUBLISHING

Published by
I-Form Ink Publishing
A division of Insu-Form, Incorporated, a California Corporation
41-921 Beacon Hill, Suite A
Palm Desert, California 92211

**Visit us on the Web! www.i-form-ink.com**
**E-mail: john@i-form-ink.com**
**Copies of this book are available at Amazon.com**

Library of Congress Control Number: 2006900908
ISBN: 0-9763274-2-2

Printed in the United States of America by Morris Publishing
3212 East Highway 30
Kearney, NE 68847
1-800-650-7888

Cover and Illustrations by Dentawa Manoi
Edited by Julie A. Gorges

# *A C K N O W L E D G M E N T S*

*I want to give credit to all my friends and acquaintances
who over the years have shared
some of these stories and jokes with me.*

*Among these are Chuck Booth, Janice Hacker, Marvin
Lindholm, Dave and Kathy Willaman, and for many of the
stories in Chapter 10, Peter Tesoro.*

*When they read the material and recognize it, I
hope they laugh and take pleasure that it is
being shared by others.*

*And thanks to my dear wife, Carmen, who has had to
listen to these stories for almost 50 years; to my children
and grandchildren, I must give a big thanks for their
patience and understanding.*

*A special thanks to Julie A. Gorges who edited
this book and to Dentawa Manoi for the artwork.*

# TABLE OF CONTENTS

# 1

# Being A Grandparent

Jerry Seinfeld makes fun of us old people in a comedy routine. Old people are always invited to wedding receptions where they dance funny, eat funny and leave early, he says. Maybe he's right. We're part of a comedy routine and don't realize it.

This is especially true when you become a grandfather. Before you know it, you're the straight man for a comedy act with your grandchildren. Naively, you don't have a clue what's coming, but before you know it everyone is laughing. Let me explain.

As a toddler, my darling little grandson, Jon, came up to me while I read my newspaper. He put a little green ball into my hand and in an innocent voice asked, "Grandpa, what is this?" I looked at it, felt it and it was kind of rubbery. But even with all my years of experience, I had to admit I didn't know what it was. "Where did you get it?" I asked him. By then we had the attention of all the family who looked on with interest.

This little sweet boy had set me up. "Out of my nose," he answered.

For the next comedy act, the whole family was sitting down at the table having dinner. Jon asked without warning, "Grandpa, what does sex mean?" Believing that I had explained this very well to my own children, I was proud to explain the facts of life to my little grandson.

I thought I did a marvelous job and my wife smiled with approval. My daughter and son-in-law looked pleased. I felt proud of myself and asked, "Do you have any questions?" Little did I know I was being set up again. He looked at me and in all innocence said, "Grandpa, how am I going to put everything you told me on this application for a library card where it says sex?"

A few days later, Jon was talking to his little friends. They were discussing where babies came from. One boy said a stork delivered babies, another said they came from the Sears catalog. Jon put them all straight. "My grandfather told me where babies come from and from what he said they are homemade."

Jon and his friends had lots of opinions about marriage. One boy said, "You got to find somebody who likes the same stuff. If you like sports, she should like it that you like sports and keep the chips and dip coming."

I asked them how old you should be before you get married. One boy said, "Twenty-three is best because you know the person forever by then." Jon added, "You got to be stupid to get married because you have to have sex with your wife. I don't want to be all grossed out. Besides, to keep her happy, you have to tell her she looks pretty even if she looks like a truck."

What'd they think about dating and kissing, I asked. One girl said, "Dates are for having fun. Even boys have something to say if you listen long enough. I think it's okay to kiss them if they're rich." A little boy said, "If you kiss someone, you should marry them and have kids with them. It's the right thing to do." My cynical grandson added, "On the first date you tell each other lies and that usually gets them interested enough to go on a second date."

I bought my grandson a pocket calculator and showed him how to use it. I then decided to give him a little test. Calculate how many seconds there are in a year." He replied, "I already know the answer." I found this hard to believe. "Okay, how many?" I asked. He answered, "Twelve. January 2nd...February 2nd..."

As a new grandparent, I took pleasure reading to Jon. As a civil engineer, I also enjoyed teaching him arithmetic. Like a typical grandparent, I started bragging how smart he was because, of course, nobody's grandchildren are as smart as your own. Jon believed me and told the teacher he was too smart for kindergarten and should go into the first grade. He could read and do math already and was wasting his time. If they didn't put him in first grade, Jon didn't want to go back to school. Of course, I got the blame for the whole problem. My daughter said I had to speak with the teacher and clear up the mess. The principal was there along with the teacher, and I explained why I felt Jon should go to the first grade. My grandson gladly demonstrated his reading and arithmetic abilities.

The principal agreed, but the woman teacher was not so easily impressed. She replied that there was more to kindergarten than reading and math. Students must also learn to reason and to think. "I will ask him two questions and see how he responds," she said. The first question was: "What does a cow have four of that a woman has two of?" Jon answered quickly, "Legs." The teacher said, "Very good." The second question: "What is in a man's pants that are not in a woman's pants?" Once again, Jon answered quickly, "Pockets." Again, she said very well and agreed that he should go to the first grade. The principal and I looked at each other. The principal said, "You better put him in the second grade because I missed those questions myself."

Later that year, the teacher decided the class should have a "Grandparent's Appreciation Night." Students talked about their grandparent's hobbies, then spelled it out loud. My hobby is to collect silly T-shirts with sayings on them. For example, *"Be Politically Correct. Do Not Call Me A Dirty Old Man. I Am A Sexy Senior Citizen."* The evening was going well until Jon explained my hobby and accidentally left out the "R" when he spelled "shirts." The teacher was embarrassed and the class started snickering. The teacher finally told Jon to go to the blackboard, think about the spelling, then try and correct the word shirts. The next little boy got up and said his grandfather's hobby was gambling. After spelling gambling, the little boy said, "My grandfather would give two to one odds that Jon is going to write something dirty on the blackboard."

One summer, the whole family went camping in the mountains. At the campgrounds there was a fiberglass outhouse. The next morning I heard a big commotion and went outside. Someone had tipped over the outhouse. My son-in-law was yelling at his two boys, Jon and Chris, demanding to know which one of them committed the foul crime. Feeling that I should show off my wisdom, I asked to talk to my grandsons. I told them the story of George Washington. "George cut down the

5

cherry tree and told the truth and later became President," I said. The story worked and the oldest confessed. My son-in-law grabbed him and gave him a good spanking. I was upset. "George Washington's father didn't spank his son when he told the truth," I said. My son-in-law answered, "George Washington's father wasn't in the tree at the time."

The next day, the women wouldn't let me use the bathroom in the motor home and I was forced to use the fiberglass outhouse. My two grandsons were still feeling mischievous and dropped a firecracker down the vent pipe. All I can say, is it was a good thing that I had my pants down, because it really gave me a start. I came running out pulling up my pants, threatening mayhem on the guilty party. My grandsons laughed and said, "It's a good thing Gramps wasn't in the motor home when he let that one."

My grandson was real proud because he had learned all the days of the week. I asked him, "Can you tell me how many days start with a "T?" My grandson replied, "Two." I said, "That's real good. Do you know what they are?" He replied, "Yes, today and tomorrow."

My little grandson asked my wife a question and when she answered it, he said, "Wow! How did you get to know all this stuff?" I decided to tease him and said,

"All grandmothers must know that stuff. They don't get to be a grandmother unless they pass the mommy test to learn it." Then my little grandson beamed and said, "I get it, if you don't pass the test you have to be a grandfather."

My grandson's pet hamster died and he and his friends were giving it a funeral. I came up just as they were finishing and heard the end to his little prayer. "In the name of the father, of the son, and in the hole he goes."

A policeman was parking his van with his K-9 partner. The dog was barking. My grandson asked, "Is that a dog you got back there?" "It sure is," the policeman replied. Puzzled, my grandson asked, "What'd he do?"

Children are real observant. I was at the park with him one day and he pointed to a man and woman standing some distance apart in the park and said they must be married. Puzzled, I asked, "How can you tell?" He answered, "Because they're yelling at the same kids." Later at school, they asked him what his parents had in common. He answered: "Both don't want any more kids."

One of my cousins liked to tease my little grandson. He would offer him the choice between a big nickel or a small dime. My grandson always chose the big nickel.

One day I asked him, "Do you realize the dime is worth more than the nickel?" He replied, "I know, but if I take the dime he'll quit giving me nickels."

One day while brushing his teeth, my grandson dropped his toothbrush into the toilet. I picked it up and threw it into the trash and told him it was not fit to use any more. He then threw my toothbrush into the trash. I asked, "Why'd you do that?" He answered, "Because it fell in the toilet last week when I went to get mine."

I overheard one of my grandson's little friends, a little girl who had just finished her first week of school, say to her mother. "I'm just wasting my time. I can't read, I can't write and they won't let me talk!"

My youngest grandson asked if it was true that from dust we come and to dust we return. I said, "Yes. Why do you ask?" He replied that he looked under his bed and either someone was coming or someone was going.

Grandchildren do not always listen well. My grandson asked, "What is marriage to one woman called?" I told him, "Monogamy." Later he told my wife that I said, "Marriage to one woman was monotony."

If someone says you're not playing with a full deck now that you're old, tell them that it's your grandchildren's fault, since they've been into your cards.

I took my little grandson to see a variety show with a ventriloquist and a puppet. He had the puppet tell one joke after another. Finally, the puppet looked at my grandson and asked, "Whose little girl are you?" My grandson was offended and yelled, "I'm not a girl. Take that back." This startled the ventriloquist who began to apologize. "This is only humor and not meant to insult anyone. Please don't take what I'm saying personally." My grandson responded, "It's not you, it's that little runt on your knee that I'm mad at."

# 2

# **Babysitting**

When a grandfather retires he's fair game to become a babysitter. However, a grandfather is probably the worst babysitter in the world.

One day my wife, daughter, grandson and I went shopping at the mall. A grandfather and three-year-old grandson have a low tolerance for shopping, so they left us at a restaurant to eat while they shopped. After a while my grandson said he had to go potty. Since I could see the restroom, I told him to go ahead. Just as my wife and daughter arrived, with perfect comedic timing, my grandson came out of the bathroom with his pants down around his ankles. Walking like a penguin and holding a piece of toilet paper in his hand, he yelled, "Grandpa, wipe me." My wife and daughter refused to help, so I ended up walking through a crowded restaurant with a bare ass kid under my arm. I tried to look dignified while everyone was laughing.

You would think I'd learn. At a girl's basketball game, he again asked to go to the bathroom. He got lost and found himself in the women's locker room. When he was spotted, the room burst into shrieks, with girls grabbing towels and running for cover. He watched in amazement and asked, "What's the matter. Haven't you ever seen a little boy before?"

One evening I was babysitting my grandsons. The boys were up in their bedroom playing and my daughter told me they were to stay in their rooms. Later, I heard one of the boys trying to sneak down the stairs. I hollered, "Get back in that room." A little later he started down the stairs again. Once again, I hollered to stay in the room. An hour later, the woman next door came over and asked if I had seen her little boy. A little voice from upstairs said, "I'm up here, but the mean Grandpa downstairs won't let me leave."

I was driving with my grandson one warm summer evening when a woman in the convertible ahead of us stood up and waved. She was stark naked. As I was reeling from the shock, I heard my five-year-old grandson shout from the back seat, "Grandpa! That lady isn't wearing a seat belt!"

While babysitting, I should have remembered my own childhood and the stupid games boys invent. For example, one day my three brothers and I got on the roof to see who could lean over the furthest. I won, which I realized after regaining consciousness.

One day my grandsons decided to see who could jump over the cactus patch. While I was taking the stickers out of my youngest grandson's rear end, I asked him why they did it. "It didn't seem like such a bad idea at the time," Chris said.

**WE AIM TO PLEASE. YOU AIM TOO, PLEASE.**

Another night while babysitting, I noticed a little puddle by the toilet. Not wanting to embarrass anyone, I put a rag in the bathroom and told my two grandsons that whoever made the mess could secretly clean it up and no one would ever know who committed the crime. We all went to separate rooms and I heard a door open and footsteps to the bathroom and back again. We all came out of our rooms and I commended my grandsons. When my wife came home, I told her how wisely I handled the problem. A few minutes later, she told me to look in the bathroom. Now there were two puddles and a little handwritten note that said, "The phantom strikes again."

I dropped my grandson at my mother's house for a few minutes while I ran on an errand. While there, my grandson saw her false teeth soaking in a glass. When I picked him up he told me what he had seen and added, "The tooth fairy will never believe this!"

When my grandsons asked me if they could build an animal trap, I should have remembered my youth. But I was watching a football game and was grateful for some time alone. Besides, it seemed like an innocent request at the time.

Their idea of an animal trap was to dig a hole under the clothesline, put sticks over it and then cover the hole with dirt. Well, the next day they caught a wild animal: my wife. I heard a scream and went outside and my dear wife was sprawled out flat on the ground with freshly washed clothes everywhere. When I discovered she wasn't hurt, I made the fatal mistake of laughing. To make matters worse, when we confronted my grandsons, they said I told them they could build the trap. My wife thinks I put them up to it. To this day, she gives me that funny look once in a while, as if she actually believes I might have tried to kill her.

Now that I wasn't trusted to be alone with my grandchildren, they hired a young girl as a babysitter. My two grandsons locked her out of the house and Jon decided to give his brother a haircut. His idea of a haircut was a modified Mohawk in the form of an arrow. When we returned, the babysitter was sitting on the porch traumatized. She never babysat again.

Since the haircut couldn't be corrected, Chris' head was shaven so he looked like an onion. My grandson noticed that he looked like me with no hair and wanted to know what happened to me. I told him my hair had moved...to my nose, my ears and somewhere else I didn't want to talk about. "Intelligent thinkers lose their hair in the front and sexy men lose their hair in the back," I added. He looked at me and said, "Grandpa, does that mean you only think you're sexy?"

A friend of mine made some homemade wine and gave me a bottle. I drank a glass and it gave me a royal headache. The next day I asked my little grandson to say grace at our meal. He blessed all the family and gave thanks for the food and then said, "God, please help grandfather not get sick from drinking too much wine."

I read the account of Adam and Eve to my grandson describing how Eve was made from one of Adam's ribs. A few days later, he came to me worried. "I have a pain in my side. Do you think I'm going to have a wife?"

15

My grandkids aren't dumb. My mother-in-law disapproved of drinking and decided to teach her great-grandchildren about the dangers of alcohol. She took them into my den, got a glass of my good scotch and another of water. She put a worm into the scotch and it shriveled up and died. She put another worm into the water and it lived. "What does that prove?" she asked the boys. Jon answered, "If you drink scotch you won't get worms."

Older brothers always find ways to torment their younger siblings. One day Jon told Chris that he was so dumb he didn't know his ass from a hole in the ground. I told Jon, "That's not a nice thing to say about your younger brother." Jon said. "I'll prove it to you." He dug two holes in the ground and told Chris he was going to give him a test to see if he was observant. He pointed to one hole and said, "This is a hole in the ground." Then he pointed to the other hole and said, "Chris, this hole is your ass. Now which one is your ass?" Chris paid close attention and proudly pointed to the second hole and said, "This hole is my ass." Jon shrugged his shoulders, looked at me and said, "See."

So it goes. For a while a younger brother believes everything his older sibling tells him. One day Chris asked if I knew anything about smart pills. Jon had given him some and he wanted to know if they worked.

Out of curiosity, I asked Chris to show them to me. "What do they remind you of?" I asked. He looked for a long time and finally said, "Rabbit droppings." I told him, "I guess they work because you're getting smarter already."

When I scolded Jon, my grandson had a question. "Rabbits and goats eat grass and they have small round poop. Cows eat the same grass and poop big, and horses again eat the same grass and have big round poop. Why is that?" I told him, "I don't know." He said, "I guess that's why great-grandma says that you don't know crap." Before I sent Jon to his room for all his antics that day, I paid my mother-in-law back for her comment. "You know they found a mother-in-law skeleton," I told Jon. "How did they know it was a mother-in-law skeleton?" he asked. "The jaws were still moving," I replied.

The Spanish have a proverb. "Bury your mother-in-law face down. That way if she talks, she just goes further down."

Jon thinks he's smart, but sometimes both of my grandsons are gullible. We took a trip to Mexico and spent the day at the beach. I rented a donkey for them and watched them ride down the beach where some Mexican boys were playing. All of a sudden they got off and went to the back of the donkey to look at something. They got back on the animal with puzzled expressions. When they returned, I asked them why they got off the donkey. "The Mexican kids kept saying, 'Here comes a donkey with two white assholes .' We had to see if it was true," Jon said.

One night while we were eating dinner, I was trying to get the ketchup to come out of the bottle when the phone rang. I asked my grandson to answer it. He then told the caller, "Grandpa can't come to the phone right now. He is hitting the bottle."

Another day I saw my little grandson sitting on the curb crying. I went over and asked him what was wrong. He replied, "I can't keep up with the big boys." I put my arm around him, sat on the curb and said, "I guess I had better cry too because I can't keep up with the big boys any more myself."

The grandkids invited a friend for dinner and as is customary in our home, we said grace. Afterwards, his friend asked them, "How come you can't eat until your grandfather reads the plate?"

My gardener cut back the shrubs and trees. His two little boys helped and piled all the branches high in the trailer and left the gate under the pile. The father was upset and told his two boys to lie on top and hold everything down while he drove a short way to dump the trash. When Chris saw this, he came running into the house excited. "Grandpa, they are throwing away two perfectly good little boys," he said.

You must realize grandsons delight in getting you in trouble. They can be first class finks. Once I made the mistake of telling Chris to pull my finger. He pulled my finger and of course I passed gas. Chris ran to Grandma as fast as he could to tattle on me. She marched into the room and said, "Good Lord, when are you going to grow up?" At Bible class the next day when they asked Chris if he knew who the Lord was, he said, "Grandpa," and told the whole story.

One day I took Chris sailing. The tide was going out. "I don't know if we can make it back since the current is so strong," I teased and started the engine. Much to my surprise, we did have a hard time getting back. The boat went real slow. Finally when we got to the dock, I said, "Chris, I thought I was only kidding when I told you we'd have a hard time getting in, but the current really fooled me." He said, "Yeah Grandpa, we would have washed out to sea for sure if I hadn't put out the anchor."

Another day, Chris asked me when I was going to move to a retirement community, Hemet, California. I wasn't planning on moving to Hemet, I told him. "Why do you ask?" Chris said he thought all old people went to Hemet. "Old people go to Sun City; their parents go to Hemet," I informed him. In fact, I overheard some old people from Hemet talking about losing their eyesight, dizzy spells and being unable to turn their heads. No wonder they have bumper stickers that say, "Pray for me, I drive in Hemet."

My grandson got a part in a school play. "I play a man who has been married for 20 years," he told me. "That's nice. Maybe next time you'll get a talking part," I replied.

My grandson was watching me dress for a party. When he saw me put on my tuxedo he warned, "Grandpa, you shouldn't wear that suit." I asked him why. He replied, "It always gives you a headache the next morning."

My wife makes the best chocolate chip cookies. Now that she watches her weight, she only bakes for special occasions. One day she made a batch of cookies for a baby shower and gave us orders that we were not to touch them. When she went to the car, my grandsons came up with a plan. "We'll watch Grandma and you can sneak us some cookies. When she starts coming back to the house, we'll warn you." I felt like a little kid again and agreed. Just as I was nabbing the cookies, Jon started yodeling for some unknown reason. My wife came in and caught me red-handed. After I got a good chewing out, I asked my grandson why he didn't warn me and he said, "Grandpa, I kept saying, here comes the old lady, old lady—hoo." I swear, if I was on my death bed and asked for cookies, my wife would say, "No, I need them all, for the gathering after your funeral."

A new teacher was trying to make use of her Psychology courses. She started her class by saying, "Anyone who thinks they are stupid, stand up!" After a few seconds, my grandson stood up. The teacher said, "Do you think you're stupid?" "No, ma'am, but I hate to see you standing there all by yourself."

My grandsons like to tell stories and even if you know the punch line you'll still say, "No why?"

Some recent examples are:

Do you know why the dummy jumped off the Empire state building? "No why?" He wanted to make a hit on Broadway.

Do you know why the dummy jumped off the Empire state building? "No why?" He wanted to show the world he had guts.

Do you know why the dummy jumped off the Empire state building? "No why?" He was smoking a cigar and threw off the wrong butt.

Do you know why the dummy always opens the screen door before he goes out? "No why?" He doesn't want to strain himself.

Do you know why the grandmother put roller skates on her rocking chair? "No why?" So she could rock and roll.

Do you know why you need a strong back to play karaoke? "No why?" Because when you give a kid from Oklahoma a piggy back ride he might be heavy.

Do you know why a man with ten children is more content than a man with a million dollars? "No why?" The man with ten children does not want any more.

Oh well. I guess if they humor me with my stories, I can humor them and listen to their jokes.

My grandson came up to me and asked, "What was your favorite fast food when you were growing up?" I informed him that I didn't have fast food when I was growing up. All we had was slow food, and it was served at a place called home. We sat down in the evening at the dinner table and we ate what your great-grandmother put on the table. Now this might be okra, turnips, eggplant, beets, cauliflower, spinach, sauerkraut, rhubarb or liver. If I didn't like what she put on my plate, I was allowed to sit there until I liked it. She used to say some child in China was starving and would love eating this food. I never understood why eating that food made any difference to a child in China.

I could have told him we had to ask permission to leave the table, but by then he was laughing so hard, I figured he couldn't handle any more childhood stories.

I overheard my little grandson using some bad words one day and gave him a lecture. I then made the mistake of comparing him to someone else: his cousin. I said. "You never hear your cousin use those words." He answered, "He does too." "Why do you say that?" I asked. He answered, "Because I taught him some yesterday."

Chris' kindergarten class was on a field trip to their local police station. They saw pictures tacked to a bulletin board of the "Ten Most Wanted" criminals. One of the youngsters pointed to a picture and asked if it really was the photo of a wanted person. "Yes," said the policeman. "The detectives want very badly to capture him." Chris asked, "Why didn't you keep him when you took his picture?"

I asked my little grandson if he knew what he wanted to be when he grew up. "What do you do, Grandpa?" he asked. I explained that I played golf, took them to the zoo, went sailing and fishing, traveled with my wife, and went to plays and concerts. He thought a minute and then answered, "I want to be a grandfather when I grow up."

Try to explain to your grandchildren why in the English language: Noses run and feet smell. You get close to close the door. You present the present at the present. You object to the object. You subject the subject. You produce produce. You bar the bar. You refuse more refuse. You turn right to be right. You let a tear cause a tear. Make out when you're out. Lead by getting the lead out. Be out when you make an out. You intimate something to your intimate friend. They can make insurance invalid to an invalid. You can desert yourself in the desert. You can cause a row when you row. We ship by truck and send cargo by ship. People recite at a play and play at a recital. How do you race the human race? How can fat chance and slim chance be the same? How can a house burn up when it burns down?

As grandparents, we now can listen to our children educate our grandchildren with these scientific facts: IRONY: "Keep laughing and I'll give you something to cry about." OSMOSIS: "Shut your mouth and eat your dinner." CONTORTIONISM: "Will you look at that dirt on the back of your neck?" STAMINA: "You'll sit there until all that spinach is finished." WEATHER: "It looks like a tornado swept through your room." PHYSICS PROBLEMS: "If I yelled because a meteor was coming towards you, would you listen then?" THE CIRCLE OF LIFE: "I brought you into this world. I can take you out."

BEHAVIOR MODIFICATION: "Stop acting like your father!" ENVY: "There are millions of children in this world who don't have wonderful parents like you do."

I was talking to the neighbor's wife, when my little grandson came up and started pulling on my coat. Chris said he had something to tell me. I had taught him that children should never interrupt an adult when they were talking, so I told him to wait. When I finished, I asked, "What was so important?" Chris replied, "Grandpa, your fly is open."

# 3

# When Grandkids Become Teens

As time goes by, grandchildren become teenagers and the fun continues.

Jon's cousin, not the most beautiful of girls, was getting ready for a party. She had bought a party dress and the adults were telling her how nice she looked. Poor thing made the mistake of asking my ornery grandson if he thought she was pretty. Jon replied, "Yes, you're pretty: pretty fat, pretty ugly, and pretty apt to stay that way." Party dress and all, she jumped on him and started beating him. I broke up the fight and told Jon to apologize. "I'm sorry," Jon told his cousin. "Do you really mean it?" she asked. Jon, always the troublemaker, replied, "Yes, I'm sorry you're fat and ugly." She jumped on him again and this time I didn't interfere.

My grandson wanted to join the band in high school, so I gave him my old tarnished saxophone. I told him to polish it, but he was lazy and kept putting the chore off. Finally, the band teacher told Jon he couldn't stay in the band if he didn't clean up his sax.

He told the band director that dirty sax was better than no sax at all. Of course, he was kicked out of the band. He then lamented that if he had stayed in the band he might have been a world class saxophone player. I answered, "Yes, except for one thing. You don't have any talent."

Jon became old enough to get a driver's license. His father told him to improve his grades, do his chores and cut his hair. Then he could have his license. He did better in school and with his chores, but he didn't want to cut his hair. Jon came to me and said his father was being unreasonable. He argued that all his friends had long hair and besides, even Jesus Christ had long hair. I told him, yes, Jesus had long hair and he walked everywhere.

He got the point and finally cut his hair. He began studying the driving manual for the written test. While reviewing the questions with him, I asked, "What does a yellow light mean?" Chris, who was listening, said, "I know. For Grandma it means stop, for Grandpa it means speed up."

Jon got his learners permit and I rode with him in the passenger's seat while he was learning to drive. He finally got his driver's license and invited me to go for a drive. Instead of sitting in the front seat, I sat in the back.

Jon was pleased and said that I must feel so secure that I didn't find it necessary to sit in the front any more. I explained, "Now that you can drive, I want to return a favor and do to you what you did to me all those years. I want to sit in the rear and kick the back of the seat while you drive."

A younger friend of mine told me that he believed that life begins when your last child leaves home and takes the dog with him. He has so much to learn.

Grandfathers gain teenage grandsons and lose their tools. I'd accuse my grandsons of taking my shovels, but the only thing they use them for is to lean on. I have come to believe that somewhere in the world someone has millions of lost shovels. What he is doing with them is anybody's guess.

I used to say that the older I get, the better I become. The truth is, I am not half the man I used to be and never was. I tell my grandchildren that while there may be winter on the roof, there is summer in the heart. I went hiking with them, and they finally told me that if I didn't get some spring in my step, we would be there until fall.

My wife was putting on cold cream and my younger grandson asked why. I replied, "So she will stay beautiful." A little while later as she was taking it off with a tissue, he asked, "Why is she taking it off?" Before

I could say anything, Jon had to add, "Maybe she is giving up."

Remember, teenagers think differently. I showed Jon a glass of water and then drank half. "An optimist says the glass is half full and a pessimist says it's half empty," I told him. "Do you agree?" He replied, "If that's all the water you're going to drink, you should use a smaller glass."

Do you sometimes feel you should send a note with your grandson to school saying, "The opinions expressed by this child are not necessarily those of his grandfather?"

Things to think about:

- You are so delighted when during the first three years of your grandchildren's life they learn to walk and talk. Then you wonder why your children spend the next 16 years telling your grandchildren to just sit down and shut up.

- Grandchildren are God's reward for not killing your own children.

- Grandchildren seldom misquote you. In fact, they usually repeat word for word what you shouldn't have said.

- Grandchildren are honest and tell it like it is. I went to the store to get some beer and took my grandson with me. As we were leaving my wife asked if I would pick up a gallon of soy milk. Of course, I forgot. When we got home, she asked if I got the soy milk.  To stay out of trouble, I replied "I couldn't find it." My grandson had to add, "Grandpa we didn't look for soy milk."

- If you have a lot of tension and you get a headache, do what it says on the aspirin bottle: "Take two aspirin." and "Keep away from children."

- It doesn't help to child-proof your home, because they will still get in.

I went to a PTA meeting with my grandson and the only seats available were in the front row.  The principal began to give a long winded, boring talk and I fell asleep and began to snore quite loudly.  Finally, the principal stopped talking and asked my grandson to wake me up. My grandson answered, "No way, you wake him up. You're the one who put him to sleep."

ADVISE FOR THE DAY.  Be nice to your kids. They will choose your nursing home.

# 4

# Being a Macho Man in Modern Times

We are told that we should make love not war, but you can get married and do both. I love being married. It's great to find that one special person you want to annoy for the rest of your life.

An old fashioned marriage doesn't make for the best of friends. We were given bad advice on how to treat our wives by the old men of our time. We were told, "Keep them barefoot and pregnant," and have the attitude, "Me Tarzan, you Jane." We had to learn the hard way. Confucius says, "Man who fight all day get no peace at night."

Old television programs, like "Father Knows Best" and "Leave It to Beaver" used to have these perfect families. A more realistic program would have been "The Tator Family." Dick Tator would play the domineering father, nagged by his wife, Aggie Tator, who was copied by her daughter, Emma Tator, and a son, Spec Tator, who would become a chip off the old block – a regular Tator chip – and stirring up the pot would be the mother-in-law, Ira Tator.

The comedians of the time were Machos with jokes like: "Who was that lady I saw you out with last night?" "That was no lady. That was my wife."

The politicians were no better. A woman colleague told Churchill in the House of Commons, "If I was your wife I would feed you poison." He replied, "If I was your husband, I would take the poison."

Or maybe you heard about the story of the farmer who was taking his new wife home in a horse-drawn buggy. The horse stopped. In a kind voice, the farmer asked the horse to continue. The horse refused. The farmer said "That is one," and waited. His patience impressed his wife. The horse finally started again, but after a while stopped. The farmer once again asked the horse to continue and the horse refused. "That's two," the farmer said. Again, he waited patiently. When the horse stopped a third time and refused to continue he said, "That's three," and took out his gun and shot the horse. When his wife criticized him for shooting the horse, he smiled and said, "That's one."

Professor Higgins of "My Fair Lady" explained it in his song, "Why can't a woman be more like a man?"

Why is putting down the toilet seat such a big thing? Men need it up, women need it down. Men don't complain about women leaving it down. At night, women may sit on the porcelain, but men pee on the lid.

Why do women ask a question they really do not want an answer to? Like asking if we think you're fat. There isn't an answer that won't make you mad. Besides, if you have to ask, you probably are.

All men see only primary colors. Don't buy us any ties that are color coordinated to a special shirt. We will always put on a different one and you will get upset. Our taste is in our mouth and that is where we want to keep it.

Do not tell us you do not have anything to wear. Remember we see your closet. We feel that you already have enough clothes and too many shoes. Besides, when we go somewhere, anything you wear is fine; it's us you have to worry about.

Remember men are like monkeys, if it itches we will scratch it, and the one who snores will always fall asleep first, and it is usually the man.

We went to Australia and happened onto a nude beach. Of course, my wife was shocked and told me to stop looking at the naked women. "I'm old, not dead," I told her. She replied that the good Lord would strike me blind if I kept looking. "Okay, then, I'll close one eye and take my chances with the other," I answered.

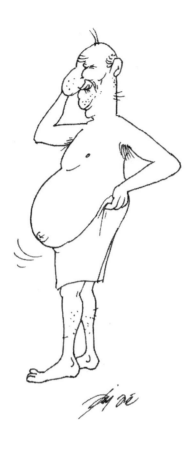

You could not pay an old woman enough money to go around the house in her bloomers. However, an old man thinks it's neat to parade around the house in his underwear. A word of caution, he should wear boxer shorts. If someone comes, they can be turned sideways so as not to embarrass anybody.

We have seen quite a change with the woman's lib movement. As a result, if an old man makes advances on a younger woman it's called "sexual harassment." When a younger woman makes a pass at an older man, it's called, "Just lucky."

While gossiping, you can use the telephone, the telegraph or even the television, but the oldest and fastest way of spreading gossip, is tell-a-woman.

Statistics show that at the age of 70 there are five women for every man. With those odds some macho men really take advantage. Like the ad I saw for a wife. "Wanted, for romance and marriage: a lady with a sailboat who loves sailing, fishing and traveling. Please send a picture of the boat."

I met an old classmate who I hadn't seen in many years and asked him if he married his sweetheart from school. He said yes, and added that they were going to celebrate their 50th anniversary. I asked him what he planned to do. He replied, "Well, for our 25th I took her back east to see her mother. For our 50th I guess I'll go back and get her."

A man marries a woman to "become as one" and trouble starts when they try to decide which one.

Another friend was going to celebrate his 50th and his wife told him a little secret. "Honey, ever since we were first married, I put a dollar in a savings account every time we made love, and guess what? We now have enough money to take a two-week vacation to Hawaii." He looked at her and replied, "That's nice. Now here's my little secret. I put a dollar in a savings account every time you didn't want sex, and now we have enough money to take a trip around the world."

An older couple was on an airliner when a man next to them asked where they were from. The husband answered, "Boise, Idaho, have you ever been there?" The man replied, "I stopped there once and ate at a restaurant where I was served by the rudest, most obnoxious old waitress I have ever met." The wife, somewhat deaf, asked, "What did he say?" Her husband replied, "He says he met your mother."

Why do many couples marry for better, or for worse, but not for good?

Fifty Years of Trying to Understand Women:

- A man will pay $2 for a $1 item he needs. A woman will pay $1 for a $2 item she doesn't need.

- A woman worries about the future until she gets a husband. A man never worries about the future until he gets a wife. A successful man is one who makes more money than his wife can spend. A successful woman is one who can find such a man.

- To be happy with a man you must understand him a lot and love him a little. To be happy with a woman you must love her a lot and not try to understand her at all.

- Any married man should forget his mistakes— there's no use in two people remembering the same thing.

- Married men live longer than single men, but it may only seem that way.

- Men wake up as good-looking as they went to bed. Women somehow deteriorate during the night.

- A woman marries a man expecting he will change, but he doesn't. A man marries a woman expecting that she won't change and she does.

- A woman has the last word in any argument. Anything a man says after that is the beginning of a new argument.

We always hear "the rules" from the female side. Here are the rules from the old macho side. (Young men don't dare use them since they'd end up sleeping on the couch. But young men shouldn't let that bother them. We learned by experience, it's just like camping.)

- Crying is blackmail. Ask for what you want. Be clear on this one: Subtle hints do not work. Strong hints do not work. Obvious hints do not work. Just say it!

- If you ask a question you don't want an answer to, expect an answer you don't want to hear. "Yes" and "No" are perfectly acceptable answers to almost every question. Come to us with a problem only if you want help solving it. That's what we do.

- Anything we said six months ago is inadmissible in an argument. In fact, all comments become null and void after seven days. If something we said can be interpreted two ways and one of the ways makes you sad or angry, we meant the other one. If we ask what is wrong and you say "nothing," we will act like nothing's wrong. We know you are lying, but it is just not worth the hassle.

- You can either ask us to do something or tell us how you want it done. Not both. If you already know best how to do it, just do it yourself.

"Bigamy is having one wife too many. Monogamy is the same." (Oscar Wilde)

You know you are an old married man when:

- You don't care where your spouse goes shopping, just as long as you don't have to go along.
- Getting a little action means you don't need fiber today.
- Getting lucky means you find your car in the parking lot.
- An all-nighter means not getting up to pee.
- You learn that a successful marriage isn't finding the right person; it's being the right person.

An elderly man in Florida owned a large farm for several years. He had a large pond in the back fixed up nice; picnic tables, horseshoe courts, and some apple and peach trees. The pond was properly shaped and used for swimming when it was built. One evening, the old farmer decided to go down to the pond since he hadn't been there for a while, and look it over. He grabbed a five-gallon bucket to bring back some fruit. As he neared the pond, he heard voices shouting and laughing with glee. As he came closer he saw it was a bunch of young women skinny-dipping in his pond. He made the women aware of his presence and they all went to the deep end. One of the women shouted to him, "We're not coming out until you leave!" The old man frowned, "I didn't come down here to watch you ladies swim naked or make you get out of the pond naked." Holding the bucket up he said, "I'm here to feed the alligator."

Moral: Old men can still think fast.

My wife said women aren't stupid and showed me an article in the newspaper. A reporter was interviewing some women in Afghanistan. The reporter asked why they still walked several paces behind the men now that they had been liberated. Their answer was simple, "Landmines."

Sally was driving home from one of her business trips in Northern Arizona when she saw an elderly

Navajo woman walking on the side of the road. As the trip was a long and quiet one, she stopped the car and asked the Navajo woman if she would like a ride. With a word or two of thanks, she got in the car. After resuming the journey and a bit of small talk, the Navajo woman noticed a brown bag on the seat next to Sally. "What's in the bag?" asked the old woman. Sally looked down at the brown bag and said, "It's a bottle of wine. I got it for my husband." The Navajo woman was silent for a moment, and then speaking with the quiet wisdom of an elder said, "Good trade."

I am a skinny person and irritated my wife when I said, "You know, sometimes I forget to eat." She replied, "Now I've forgotten my address, my mother's maiden name, and my keys. But I've never forgotten to eat. It's just stupid to forget to eat." It seems the older you get, the tougher it is to lose weight because by then, your body and your fat are really good friends.

One day a couple of clean-cut young people came to my door and I invited them in. They told me that God was going to destroy all the wicked and make the earth a paradise, and all us old people would be young again. My wife heard this and stuck her head through the door and said, "Can you imagine having to put up with him for eternity? He's lived long enough now to know better, but if he's young again, he'll probably do it anyway."

With that in mind, here are some rebuttals from my wife:

- On anniversaries, the wise husband may forget the past, but he should never forget the present.
- A foolish husband says to his wife, "Honey, you stick to the washing, ironing, cooking and scrubbing. No wife of mine is going to work."
- If a man has enough horse sense to treat his wife like a thoroughbred, she will never turn into an old nag.
- Behind every successful woman is herself. I have yet to hear a man ask for advice on how to combine marriage and a career.
- Whether a man winds up with a nest egg or a goose egg depends a lot on the kind of chick he marries.
- Trouble in marriage often starts when a man gets so busy earning his salt that he forgets his sugar.
- If you want breakfast in bed, sleep in the kitchen.

Men may say, "I thought real happiness was getting married and then it was too late." However, a study indicated that while 80 percent of husbands say they would remarry their wives, only 50 percent of the women said they would remarry their husbands.

CHAPTER

# 5

# Doctor Visits

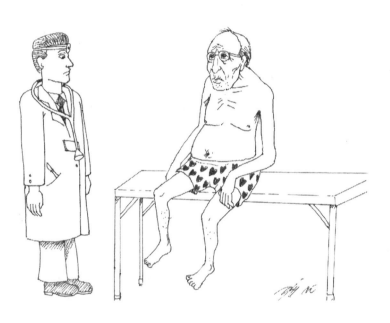

*"IF I HAD KNOWN THAT I WAS GOING TO LIVE THIS LONG, I WOULD HAVE TAKEN BETTER CARE OF MYSELF."*

At my age, when I fill out an application that asks who to notify in case of an emergency, I feel like writing, "A good doctor."

My wife works to stay fit and at her last checkup came out very happy. When I asked why, she replied that the doctor had told her that her breasts were like those of a woman 10 years younger. Teasing her, I asked, "But what did he say about your old ass?" She replied, "I'm sorry, we didn't talk about you."

I went in for my physical and as typical of a man my age, my blood pressure and cholesterol were too high. The doctor said if I didn't make some changes, I could have a heart attack. Since the doctor was a friend of mine, I asked him to tell my wife that she needed to prepare me three nutritious meals every day, not upset me and give me lots of loving. My wife went in and I waited outside. When she came out, I asked what the doctor said. "That you are going to die," she replied.

A friend of mine went to the doctor and said he had a problem: he had a bowel movement every morning at 6:00 a.m. The doctor replied that was good for his age. My friend replied, "Not when you don't wake up until 7:00 a.m."

If you go to the doctor and tell him your left arm hurts and he can't figure out why, he'll say it's just old age. I don't buy that because my right arm is just as old and it doesn't hurt.

Of course, being over the hill is much better than being under it.

Old people do have pain; however, they learn to live with it. An old man slipped on a patch of ice and landed flat on his back. When a younger person asked, "Does it hurt?" He looked up and said, "Only when I laugh."

As you age, the doctor will eventually recommend a colonoscopy. Forget about your dignity. You feel like asking, "Are we there yet, are we there yet, are we please there yet?" Of course, you can ask the doctor to give you a note for your mother-in-law stating that he didn't find your head in there.

One thing that happens to older men is that everything they eat turns to gas. If a group of men are together and one has gas, no problem. He doesn't even need to excuse himself; he just lets it fly and then proudly dedicates it, "Here is a one gun salute for the football team that left town."

Women are another story. Of course, gas problems are not as bad for women. Since they talk most of the time, they let out a lot of hot air. (The statistics bear this out; women speak 7000 words a day while a man speaks 2000.) However, if they do have gas, they always try to hide the fact. If a man goes into a room full of women and one of the lovely ladies has flatulence, he had better say, "Excuse me," because he's going to get the blame anyway.

I got sick and my daughter offered to take me to the doctor. My two grandchildren were concerned because I am rarely sick. They got in the back with two pillows, and as I leaned one way, they propped me up with a pillow. When I leaned the other way, they propped me up with the other pillow. It wasn't until we got to the doctors office and I got out of the car that I was able to get rid of the gas killing me.

Of course, boys are fascinated with this bodily function and although in my youth we had some interesting experiences lighting matches to gas, I decided not to share this fact with my grandsons. I could just picture the older grandson burning all the hair off his brother's ass and saying, "Grandpa told us we could."

My wife asked me the other day why I didn't have this gas problem while we were courting. I was good at hiding the problem back then, I told her. If it was any consolation, I would never leave her because now I can't hold them long enough to fool another woman.

Once I asked the doctor about my gas problem. "At least they're silent," I said adding that I had just passed some gas while sitting there. "What should I do?" I asked. The doctor replied, "The first thing we should do is test your hearing."

Old people don't do drugs. We get the same effect just standing up fast.

An elderly gentleman of 85 feared his wife was getting hard of hearing. The doctor made an appointment for a hearing test in two weeks, but meanwhile said there was a simple informal test the husband could try. "Stand about 40 feet away from her and speak in a normal conversational tone and see if she hears you," the doctor instructed. "If not, go to 30 feet, then 20 feet, and so on until you get a response."

That evening, the wife was in the kitchen cooking dinner. The husband was about 40 feet away in the living room. In a normal tone he asked, "Honey, what's for supper?" No response. So the husband moved 10 feet closer and repeated, "Honey, what's for supper?" Still, no response. Next he moved into the dining room about 20 feet from his wife and asked, "Honey, what's for supper?" Again, no response. So he walked up to the kitchen door, only 10 feet away. "Honey, what's for supper?" Again, there was no response. So he walked right up behind her. "Honey, what's for supper?" "Damn it, for the fifth time, CHICKEN!"

He then went to the doctor for a complete physical. He was asked to provide a urine sample, a stool sample and a semen sample. The old man said, "What?" His wife said loudly, "He wants your shorts."

Never take life seriously. Nobody gets out alive anyway and health is merely the slowest possible rate at which one can die.

The doctor examined an old man who had an enlarged prostrate. He told him that it would affect his sex life. The old man said, "Which part, the thinking about it or the talking about it?"

An old man at the bar kept ordering straight whiskey with two drops of water. When asked by the bartender why, he answered, "I can hold my liquor but my water is something else."

An older couple was watching TV and an evangelist told everyone if they wanted to be healed to place one hand on the TV and the other hand on the body part they wanted cured. The old woman slowly hobbled to the TV, placed one of her hands on the TV and the other on her arthritic shoulder. The old man went to the TV, placed his right hand on the set and his left hand on his crotch. The wife looked at him and said, "You don't understand. This is to heal, not raise the dead."

When you get older, what you want and what you get are two different things. For breakfast what I want is: ham and eggs, biscuits with butter, fried potatoes and gravy. What I get is all-bran, soy milk, dry toast and a lecture on cholesterol.

When two old people decide to get married, they should list the local pharmacy as the bridal registry.

They say a dog is good for your health. My wife heard of a dog that was up for adoption and had been taught to pray. I was skeptical and went down to see. When they said pray, the dog bent his rear legs, put his two front paws together, lowered his head and barked softly. My wife wanted the dog. When we got home I thought I would see if the dog would obey other commands. I took him out for a walk and said, "Heel." He jumped up, put both paws on my forehead, put his head back, closed his eyes and started barking at the heavens. I then realized that I had an evangelic dog.

As we get older we sometimes become a little stubborn. An old man was going to Chicago from Los Angeles and had never flown before. When he got on the plane he picked a seat and sat down. The flight attendant told him he was in the wrong seat. He had always ridden on buses where you picked your own seat and said he would not move until he got to Chicago. Nobody could get him to move. Finally, the flight attendant asked the pilot if he could help. The pilot walked up and said a few words. The old man jumped up and went to his assigned seat. The flight attendants were impressed and asked the pilot what he had said. He replied, "Simple. I told him that seat was not going to Chicago."

We are told to exercise, but now we don't pump iron, we pump rust, and while we still have a little something on the ball we are just too tired to bounce.

When I was young, I thought it would be great if I looked like James Gardner and my wife looked like Elizabeth Taylor. Now I'm not so sure.

Abraham Lincoln is dead, Moses is dead and I don't feel so hot myself. Maybe that is why we older people read the Bible so much. We are cramming.

Drive carefully. It's not only cars that can be recalled by their maker.

Could it be that many of our health problems are of our own doing? We have "Angels Food" cake that is light and good and one made out of chocolate called "Devil's Food." That should tell us something.

The battle between good and evil has waged since the beginning of time. God provides good things for us and the Devil provides bad things for us.

God created fresh fruits and vegetables for healthy nutrition, so we could live healthy lives. The Devil took the wheat and made white flour and from the cane made white sugar. From these he made cakes, donuts and other sweet things that make us fat and rots our teeth.

God provided olive oil in which to cook our vegetables. He provided the potato with its healthy skin and nutritious center for us to bake slowly. The Devil took the fat from pigs and made lard in which to deep fry the potato and threw away the skin, took the starchy center and made French fries and potato chips, all soaked in grease. And he called it, "fast food."

God made the sunrise, the sunset, beautiful skies and parks, so we could get out and walk and play in the fresh air. The Devil made television with remote controls and hundreds of channels so we could become couch potatoes and sit there and become, as one comedian said many years ago, people with cantaloupe eyes and no brains.

An older citizen called his doctor and was very concerned. "Is it true that the medication you prescribed has to be taken for the rest of my life?" he asked. "Yes, I'm afraid so," the doctor told him. There was a moment of silence before the senior replied, "I am wondering then, just how serious is my condition, because this prescription is marked 'NO REFILLS'."

# CHAPTER

# 6

# Old People Need Loving Too

George Burns used to say he got sex almost every night, almost on Monday, almost on Tuesday…

A lecturer at a senior center contended that a positive happy outlook depended on the amount of sex you had. To prove the point, he asked those that got sex more than once a week to stand up. Several did with smiles and grins, happy people. He asked the same question with longer lengths of time, and as the various groups stood up, they became more and more reserved. The last group was grim and not too enthusiastic. He finally said, "Is there anyone here who gets sex only once a year?" An old man in the back jumped up with great enthusiasm, laughing and extremely happy. The lecturer was puzzled and asked, "Are you sure you get sex only once a year?" The old man replied, "Yes, and tonight's the night."

Two unrelated seniors, a man and a woman, had to share a sleeping compartment on a train in Europe.

During the night, the man who was on the top bunk got cold and asked the woman below if she would hand him a blanket from the closet. She replied, "Let's pretend we are married." He said, "You mean, I can sleep with you?" "No" she said. "You can get your own blanket."

For us old duffers foreplay is a half hour of begging. Of course, the spirit may be willing, but the flesh is weak. By the time we get in the mood, it's time to pee. To add insult to injury, some comedian on TV says old men have to take a half a Viagra pill every day so as to not ruin their shoes.

Actually, it all started in the Garden of Eden because God gave man and the animals only 20 years of sex. Man used his up and then talked the horse out of 10 years, the monkey out of 10 years and the parrot out of 10 years. As a result, every man has 20 years of sex, monkeys around for 10 years, horses around for another 10 years and, when he gets to our age, he talks about it for 10 years.

After Eve was deceived by the snake and ate the fruit, Adam tried to blame everything on her. He told God, "I listened to her because she is so beautiful. So why did you make her so beautiful?" God answered, "So you would love her." Adam asked, "But why did you make her so gullible?" God answered, "So she would love you."

What every man thinks he wants in a woman would have cost Adam an arm and a leg, not just a rib.

Every man is incomplete until he gets married and then he is finished.

When a woman says, "Go ahead," this is a dare, not permission. Don't do it. Remember, while marriages may be made in heaven, they have to be maintained on earth.

It has been said that God created the heavens and earth, then man, then rested. Then He created woman and since then no one has rested.

King Solomon proved that even the wisest of men can be stupid in their old age when it comes to women. The Bible says he had 300 wives and 700 concubines. He got in trouble with God when he let some of them make alters to their pagan gods to pray.  I can just imagine what they were praying for.

Here are a few of Solomon's observations about women. Judge for yourself what he meant.

- Proverbs 5:18: Rejoice with the wife of your youth, a lovable hind and a charming mountain goat.
- Proverbs 11:22: Like a ring of gold in the nose of a pig, is a beautiful woman who has no sense.
- Proverbs 21:9: It is better to be living in an angle of the house-top, than with a bitter-tongued woman in a wide house.

Of course, there is no fool like an old fool. An acquaintance of mine lost his wife and after a while started bar-hopping. My friend thought he would be more successful with the ladies if he dressed so he wouldn't look like an old man. He got an open neck silk shirt with a large gold chain, bell bottom pants, and since he was bald, he got an Elvis-style wig. It worked. He no longer looked like an old man. He looked like an old woman.

At another bar, he saw an attractive middle-aged woman and asked if he could buy her a drink. She said sure, but wanted him to know up front that she was a lesbian. The old codger had been out of touch so long he assumed that she was a member of some kind of new religion. "It doesn't matter," he said. Finally, after a few drinks he asked her, "By the way, what's a lesbian?" She replied, "See that woman over there. I would like to kiss her and make love to her. What do you think of that?" He looked at the woman and said, "Well, I guess I must be a lesbian too."

When an old man brags about how he gets super sex, what he really means is that he is getting soup.

A lot of old men's salvation is Viagra. My friend finally talked a younger woman into marrying him. He bragged that he was really enjoying marriage now since he got sex every day and twice on Sunday. I saw him a few months later and he looked thin and haggard. I told him he had better slow down or he was going to kill himself. A few weeks later I saw him again and he looked better. I said, "I see you took my advice." He replied, "No, I just gave up my mistress."

In my opinion, Viagra's promises are deceptive. The doctors say it makes you good for an hour, but they don't tell you where you can find a woman who is going to let you fool around for an hour.

My friend's young wife eventually made his life miserable. As a result, he started going to bars and coming home drunk and she'd pound on him. One night, she decided to try something different. She hugged and kissed him and told him, "Let's go to bed, honey." He replied, "Might as well, my wife is going beat me up when I get home anyway."

As could be expected, the divorce lawyer took him to the cleaners. His only defense was that his young wife acted like a child. The only demand the judge didn't give his wife was that my friend rot in hell for all eternity. He went to the bar to drown his troubles and after a few drinks said out loud, "Lawyers are bastards." A man at the end of the bar said, "I resent that." The old man said, "I'm sorry, are you a lawyer?" The man replied, "No, I am a bastard."

People our age can still enjoy an active, passionate sex life—provided we get cable or that dish thing.

An old man was having a drink at a bar with a younger man who was lamenting that every time he came home late, no matter how careful he was—coasting into the garage, removing his shoes, tip toeing up the stairs, sitting down to pee, and being very careful as he was getting into the bed—his wife always woke up and gave him hell. The older man shared his wisdom. He told the young man, "Make all the noise you want and when you get into bed, whisper, 'Honey, do you feel horny?' I guarantee she will pretend she is asleep."

He added another suggestion. "If your wife is asleep and her mouth is open, drop in an aspirin. When she gags and wakes up and asks what you're doing, tell her it's for her headache. If she says she doesn't have a headache, you got her."

An old farmer at the state fair had just won a blue ribbon for his prize bull. He was standing by the corral when an older, painted-up woman came up. She asked, "Why did he win the prize?" The farmer replied, "The calves he produces will later be excellent milk producers and dairy farmers will come from miles around and pay big money to have this bull inseminate their cows." She then asked, "How do they know when a cow is ready?" The farmer replied, "The cow gives off a scent that the bull can smell." As the woman started to leave, she said, "Thanks for the information and I hope your sinuses clear up."

An old couple promised that whoever went first would let the other one know what it was like. The old boy died and after a little while the woman went to a medium to have a séance and contact him. The medium told the wife that her husband said, "I have sex in the morning when I wake up, go out on the golf course, then come back and have sex, have a bite to eat, and have sex, go back out on the golf course for a while, come back and have sex…It's like that all day every day." The wife said, "Sex and golf, he must be in heaven." The medium replied, "No, he says he is a rabbit on a golf course in Arizona."

In China many years ago, the Emperor passed a law that whoever stepped on his shadow would be punished and forced to marry a very ugly person. One of his old ministers was always flattering the Emperor so as to gain favor. One day, the Emperor called him in and presented him with a beautiful young woman to be his wife. He was so proud until he found out she had stepped on the Emperor's shadow.

Two old people were talking. The man asked his wife, "What happened to our sexual relations?" She replied, "I don't know. They haven't sent us any Christmas cards in years."

ADVISE: The bonds of matrimony are a good investment only when the interest is kept up.

How old Macho men view romance:

Smart man + smart woman = romance

Smart man + dumb woman = affair

Dumb man + smart woman = marriage

Dumb man + dumb woman = pregnancy

Actually, the story of the old man and the frog fits us old guys. An old man was walking in the forest when a frog spoke to him and said, "Kiss me and I will turn into a beautiful young maiden." The old man picked up the frog and put it into his pocket. The frog once again said, "You don't understand, kiss me and I will turn into a beautiful young maiden." The old man took out the frog and said, "At my age, I would rather have a talking frog."

# 7

# I Worry About My Short Memory...But Not for Long

We've all had the experience of going into a room and not remembering why we're there. It seems our memory has moved to our ass, because when we go back and sit down, we remember. That's why old women can't have babies; they'd put the infant down and forget where they left it.

A couple I know became frustrated because they were constantly forgetting things. They decided to go to a therapist to see if he could help them with their memory. He recommended they write everything down. However, the old man was too proud to do it. One night, his wife wanted a glass of white wine. She said, "Write it down, so you don't forget." He refused and returned with coffee. His wife scolded him and said, "I told you to write it down. I asked for tea."

An old man bragged to his friend about going to a great memory class. His friend asked where the class was held. The old man thought and thought and then finally asked, "What is the name of that opera with a Spanish woman's name?" His friend answered, "You mean, Carmen?" The old man nodded, then turned to his wife and asked, "Carmen dear, where is that memory class we went to?"

A woman came up to me and asked if I had driven a school bus at the local school some 50 years ago. I had driven a school bus part-time while going to college, so I asked. "Did I drive your child to school?" Talk about sticking both feet in your mouth and not having a leg to stand on. She replied, "No, you drove me."

If you see an old friend and can't remember his name, admitting you have memory problems, you might ask, "I'm sorry, but what is your name?" Don't be surprised if your friend asks, "How soon do you need to know?"

An elderly gentleman well-dressed—flower in his lapel, hair groomed, great looking suit, smelling slightly of a good after shave, presenting a well looked after image—walked into an upscale cocktail lounge. Seated at the bar was an elderly looking lady. The gentleman walked over, sat alongside her, ordered a drink, took a sip, turned to her and said, "So, tell me, do I come here often?"

Two old men were sitting at a bar and one turned to the other and asked, "Do I know you?" The other man said, "I don't know, but you look familiar. Where'd you come from?" The first man replied, "Dublin, Ireland." The other said, "That's amazing because I'm from Dublin too. Where'd you go to school?" The first man said, "Saint Mary's." The second man said, "Me too. I graduated in 1950." The first old man replied, "That's when I graduated." Another man sitting at the bar turned to the bartender and said, "That's quite a coincidence that they'd meet after all these years." The bartender answered, "Don't pay any attention to the O'Brian twins when they've been drinking."

A friend of mine always called his wife loving nicknames—honey, my love, darling, sweetheart, cupcake, etc. They had been married almost 60 years and clearly were still very much in love. I told him, "I think it's wonderful that after all these years, you still call your wife those loving pet names." He replied, "To tell you the truth, I forgot her name about ten years ago."

If you think you can't change the past, try writing your memoirs. We sometimes remember things the way we wish they were. Wouldn't it be nice if whenever we messed up our life, we could simply press 'Ctrl Alt Delete' and start all over?

The older generation has been labeled as the silent generation; maybe they have a lot to be silent about. Sometimes, I think, a good conscience may be the result of a poor memory.

Three elderly ladies were sitting together in their rocking chairs when one said, "I'm a little hungry. I'm going in the kitchen and get some cookies and milk." When she got to the kitchen door, she turned around and asked, "Was I going in the kitchen or was I coming out?" The second one replied, "Oh my, she is getting so forgetful she makes me chilly. I think I'll go upstairs and get my sweater." She got half way up the stairs and turned and asked, "Was I going upstairs or coming down?" The third one quit rocking and responded, "My, my, I'm glad I'm not so old that I can't keep things straight. I guess I should knock on wood." [Knock, knock] "Was that the front door or was that the back one?"

Sometimes loss of memory isn't a bad thing. An old man went fishing. When he was done, he put his fish in a bucket of water and was getting ready to leave the lake. The game warden stopped him and asked for his fishing license. He didn't have one. The warden told him there was a fine of $100 for each fish he had caught. "I didn't catch those fish," the old man explained. "They're my pet fish. I bring them down to swim in the lake. When I call them, they return to me." The warden was skeptical. "Prove it," he said. The old man took the bucket and threw all the fish into the lake. The warden said, "Okay, call your fish." The old man replied, "What fish?"

Two old boys at the home wanted to play some golf, but neither one could see very well. One suggested that they take old Bob because he could see like an eagle. They invited old Bob and went out on the course. The first one hit the ball and old Bob said, "Wow, that was a beauty. What a beautiful drive." The old boy asked, "How far did it go?" Old Bob said, "What go."

My wife says I never listen to her. I think that's what she said.

I went to the doctor about my loss of memory. He gave me some pills to take three times a day. If I could remember anything three times a day, I wouldn't need the pills.

These days, I spend a lot of time thinking about the hereafter. I go somewhere to get something and then wonder what I'm hereafter.

They tell you that you'll lose your mind when you grow old. What they don't tell you is that you won't miss it much.

# CHAPTER

# 8

# No Time
# To Kill

You hear young people say they are just killing time. They will learn too late that this is not the case. Time kills you.

My wife asked me to look in the obituaries and see if she died, because she woke up that morning and nothing hurt.

Old people read the obituaries in this order: People who died their age, people who died that were younger, and finally with hope, people who died that were older. Every day I beat my own previous record for number of consecutive days I have stayed alive.

An old woman of 100 was interviewed by a reporter who asked her to name one benefit of a long life. She thought for a minute and replied, "Being at peace with everyone." The reporter asked, "Why's that?" The old lady answered, "Because I've outlived everyone who irritated me."

A senior citizen was driving down the freeway and his car phone rang. His wife's voice urgently warned him, "I just heard on the radio there's a car going the wrong way just about where you are. Please be careful!" He replied, "It's not just one car...there's hundreds of them!"

When I die, I want to die like my grandfather, who died peacefully in his sleep. Not screaming like all the passengers in his car.

At my last class reunion, an attorney was trying to impress everybody and said he had married a beautiful woman and had two sons who attended Yale; one was a successful doctor and the other was a corporate executive. He turned to another classmate and asked how he had done. The classmate replied that he had never gotten married, but he did have two sons and they both became lawyers.

His wife was no better. She began bragging to another woman about her successful husband. The other woman said, "How nice." Then she talked about her wonderful children. The other woman again said, "How nice." She continued boasting about the vacations they took every year to Europe. Again, the other woman said, "How nice." Finally, the attorney's wife asked the other woman what she had done. She replied, "I work for a public relations firm and learned to say, 'How nice' instead of 'Baloney.'"

In a home for retired ministers a priest, a rabbi, and a Protestant minister were talking. Since they were so old, the three decided that maybe it would be a good idea to confess their sins. The priest confessed that since he didn't have a wife, he had gone to a house of ill repute and had sex. The rabbi confessed that he had gone to a casino and gambled. The Protestant minister admitted that he had gone to a bar and got drunk. A fourth self-righteous minister just sat there grinning. Finally, they asked him, "Don't you have any sins to confess?" He admitted he had one, but they wouldn't like it. They insisted and finally he said, "I like to gossip."

The other ministers decided to keep an eye on him. They invited the minister on their weekly fishing trip. They took a rowboat to their favorite fishing spot and after a while the priest said he was going to the car and get a different lure. He got out of the boat, walked across the water to the shore, went to the car and walked across the water. The self-righteous minister got up, stepped off the boat and sunk to the bottom. They fished him out. He didn't say a thing. After a while the rabbi said he was going to get a lure and just like the priest, walked across the water. The self-righteous minister again got up and stepped off the boat and once again, sunk to the bottom. When they fished him out again they said, "We'd better show him where those rocks are or he is going to drown himself."

Later they decided to take a trip. On the airplane, the stewardess offered them a drink. The Protestant minister was indignant and said, "I would just as soon commit fornication as to drink alcohol." The priest said, "Do we have a choice?" The gossipy minister asked, "Can I watch?"

Two old duffers were stranded on a deserted island and had given up hope of being rescued. Finally, one said maybe they should pray. Since they had never gone to church, they didn't know what to say. Finally, one said, "I used to take my mother to church on Wednesdays and I heard them praying, so I will try. Twenty-three, forty-five, sixty-seven..." The other man asked, "What kind of prayer is that? How does it end?" He replied, "Bingo."

A reporter went to a construction site and noticed three old men working hard. She interviewed the first and asked him how old he was. He said 71. The impressed reporter asked, "And to what do you credit being able to work so hard in your old age?" The old man replied that he never smoked, drank, or chased women. She went to the next old man who said he was

74 and got the same story. Turning to the last man, she asked, "Is that true for you too?" He replied, "No, I've smoked since I was 12, I drink everything in sight and I go after all the women I can." "Amazing," the reporter said. "And how old are you?" He answered, "47."

During a flood the whole family was on the roof of the house to escape the rising water. They noticed a hat going back and forth in the water and were puzzled. Then Grandma exclaimed, "It's that old fool Grandpa. He said he was going to mow the lawn today, come hell or high water."

Eventually you will reach a point when you stop lying about your age and start bragging about it.

The older we get, the fewer things seem worth waiting in line for.

Some people try to turn back their odometers with plastic surgery. Not me. I want people to know why I look this way. I've traveled a long way and some of the roads weren't paved and I don't know how I got over the hill without getting to the top.

Old oak trees were once little nuts that held their ground.

Some people live to an old age because it's illegal to kill them.

Some ways to tell if you're over the hill:

- You no longer laugh at Preparation H commercials.
- Your arms are almost too short to read the newspaper.
- You buy shoes with crepe rubber soles.
- The only reason you're still awake at 2 a.m. is indigestion.
- People ask you what color your hair used to be.
- You enjoy watching the news.
- Your car must have four doors.
- You no longer think of speed limits as a challenge.
- You have a dream about prunes.
- You browse the bran cereal section in the grocery store.
- You start worrying when your supply of Ben Gay is low.
- You think a CD is a certificate of deposit.
- You have more than two pair of glasses.
- You read the obituaries daily.
- Your biggest concern when dancing is falling.
- You enjoy hearing about other people's operations.
- You wear black socks with sandals.

- You know all the warning signs of a heart attack.
- You learn that when you lend someone $20 and never see that person again, it was probably worth it.
- Just when you were getting used to yesterday, along came today.
- You learn that there is a very fine line between genius and insanity.
- You find that the things that come to those that wait may be the things left by those who got there first.
- Your bedtime is three hours after you fall asleep in you chair watching television.
- Despite the cost of living, you have noticed how it remains so popular.
- You think this bumper sign is stupid, "Honk if you love peace and quiet."
- You think this bumper sign is pathetic, "I gave up hope, now I feel better."
- You remember Blackjack chewing gum, wax coke-shaped bottles with colored sugar water, candy cigarettes, party phone lines, metal ice trays with levers, home delivery of milk with glass bottles, cardboard stoppers and using hand signals when driving a car.

Two old geezers were sitting on the porch drinking beer. One turned to the other and asked, "Slim, I'm 73-years-old and I'm just full of aches and pains. I know you are about my age. How do you feel?" Slim said, "I feel just like a newborn babe." Rather amazed, his friend asked, "Really? A newborn babe?" "Yup," grinned Slim. "No teeth, no hair, and I think I just wet my pants."

You learn you are getting old, when everything either dried up or leaks.

# CHAPTER 9

# Growing Up In The "Good Old Days"

Old people enjoy telling their children stories about how bad they had it when they were young. They all seemed to have walked to school five miles in the snow up-hill both ways. They brag that no one locked their doors back then. The truth of the matter is, most people didn't have anything worth stealing.

I was born in a little town called Del Norte in southern Colorado. There were two groups in town: the Latinos and the Anglos. The Anglos owned the ranches and the Latinos picked the potatoes and peas.

My mother was of the Latino group and she raised me as a single parent. We were poor and lived in a little adobe house with a dirt floor, giving the term "dirt poor" true meaning. The house didn't have running water, electricity or gas. We had a pump outside to get fresh water, which we brought inside in a bucket with a dipper. Anybody who wanted a drink of water drank out of the same dipper. How we didn't all die of the plague is anyone's guess.

The Saturday night bath was an actual occurrence. We would heat water on the wood stove and hang a blanket across the corner of the room and fill up the wash tub. The mother took the first bath, then using the same water, the father bathed, followed by each child, starting with the oldest. The water was dark by the time you got to the youngest. That's why you have the saying, "Don't throw out the baby with the bath water."

The outhouse had two holes and I always wondered why. No one ever wanted to share it with me. Toilet paper was the old "Monkey Ward Catalog," which was fine until you ran out of the standard pages and had to use the slick ones. My neighbor's outhouse was real scary. I had to use it once and saw scrawled under a horizontal two-by-four at eye level as you were sitting: "You may as well sit down. Our bugs can jump this high." When my uncle dropped his wallet in an outhouse, he tied a rope around my ankles and let me down head first through the hole to pick it up. The entire time I prayed his hand wouldn't slip.

The joke of that time was that the politicians were promising, "A chicken in every pot, and two pots under every bed."

Life changed when my mother remarried a Texan. I probably got my sense of humor from him. He had played football for Texas-Tec and one of his favorite stories was about a new recruit who joined the team from California. To initiate him, they took him to a restaurant at a local hotel where they arranged a stunt with the bartender.

They told him to order a regular size Texas beer and he was served a bucket full of beer. They insisted that this was standard size in Texas since everything was big. He was dubious, but went ahead and drank it all. Beer goes through you fast (because it doesn't have to slow down to change color), so it wasn't long and he had to go real bad. Feeling the effects of all that beer, he took the wrong door and instead of going to the bathroom, he stumbled into the room with the indoor swimming pool and fell in. When my stepfather and his friends ran in, the poor soul was yelling, "Don't flush it!"

That wasn't the end of teasing him about how big things were in Texas. The recruit went turkey hunting and came back with several nice turkeys. Of course, they told him he had only shot mosquitoes. They added that mosquitoes always ate you on the spot because if they took you home, the bigger ones would steal you away.

My Uncle used to tease, "It's easy to find Texas. You just go east until you smell it and then you go south until you step in it." You can always tell a Texan, but he won't always listen.

My father had some great quotations that I never appreciated until I got older. Such as:

- Parents know many of the answers, but children don't bother to ask the questions.
- Time may be a great healer, but it's a lousy beautician.
- Wisdom comes with age but sometimes age comes alone.
- It isn't difficult to make a mountain out of a molehill; just add a little dirt.
- The best way to get even is to forget. To forgive is to set the prisoner free and then discover the prisoner was you.
- Feed your faith and your doubts will starve to death.
- God wants spiritual fruit, not religious nuts.
- Some people wear halos much too tight. Unless you can create the whole universe in six days, perhaps giving advice to God isn't such a good idea.

In the early 40's, we moved and ended up in another little town, Beaumont, located between Los Angeles and Palm Springs. For many years, a sign at the east end of the freeway read: "The Pass Gas Station" and at the west end, "Inter-clean Laxatives." This speaks for itself as to the character of the town.

School during the war years was different than now. Not only parents spanked their children, but teachers also had the privilege. In fact, any adult could beat you. What is called child abuse now was called discipline then. I'll never forget the day two young ruffians were sent to the principal office and the teacher left the classroom door open so we could hear the cries as they got paddled. If you got spanked at school and told your parents, you got another beating for embarrassing them. My father always asked me after the beating, "Are you going to do it again?" What a stupid question. What kid in his right mind would answer truthfully? If you were going to do it again, surely you'd lie.

An unknown Internet writer had the following memories:

*My Mom used to cut chicken, chop eggs and spread mayo on the same cutting board with the same knife with no bleach, but we didn't get food poisoning. She defrosted hamburger on the counter and I used to eat raw cake dough, but I can't remember getting E-coli.*

*We took gym, not P.E., and risked permanent injury with a pair of high-top Ked's instead of cross-training athletic shoes* with air cushion soles and built-in light reflectors. I can't recall any injuries, but they must have happened quite often since they tell us how much safer we are now. Every year, someone taught the whole school a lesson by running in the halls with leather soles on the hardwood floor and hitting a wet spot. If we had only known then that we could have sued the school system.

Schools didn't offer 14-year-olds condoms (we wouldn't have known what they were for anyway). A fully uniformed nurse dispensed baby aspirin and cough syrup if we started getting the sniffles. What an archaic health system.

When we think of the dangers that could have befallen us as we trekked off each day about a mile down the road to some guy's vacant lot, built forts out of branches and pieces of plywood, made trails and fought over who got to be the Lone Ranger. What was that property owner thinking, letting us play on that lot? He should have been locked up for not putting up a fence around the property, complete with a self-closing gate and an infrared intruder alarm.

We played King of the Hill on piles of gravel left on vacant construction sites and when we got hurt, Mom pulled out the 48 cent bottle of Mercurochrome and then we got our butt spanked. Now it's a trip to the emergency room, followed by a 10-day dose of a $49 bottle of antibiotics and then Mom calls the attorney to sue the contractor for leaving a horribly vicious pile of gravel where it was such a threat.

*To top it off, not a single person I knew had ever been told that they were from a dysfunctional family. How could we possibly have known that we needed to get into group therapy and anger management classes? We were obviously so duped by so many societal ills, that we didn't even notice that the entire country wasn't taking Prozac!*

*We thought we were supposed to accomplish something before we were allowed to be proud of ourselves. We must have been bored and not realized it without computers, Play Station, Nintendo, X-box or 270 digital cable stations. The term cell phone would have conjured up a phone in a jail cell and a pager was the school PA system.*

My parents told me, "When you get to my age you will understand." But they never told me what I would understand. Or, "I've told you a million times not to exaggerate." Once my mother got mad and called me a little son-of-a-bitch. I don't think she really thought about what she was saying. Another time she asked if I was born in a barn. What if I said yes? What would that say about her?

Of course, nothing changes. When I was 70 and my mother was in her 90s, I told her she needed to go to a nursing home. She got angry and told me she didn't need a snotty nose kid telling her what to do.

In the classroom, we weren't always kind or politically correct. One day, a girl didn't know the answer to a question and was beating around the bush. The kind teacher said, "Well, you're on the right track." One of the students said, "But she is going the wrong way."

We were also sexist. A girl came to school wearing a tight sweater. The boys had a private joke. They compared girls' breast sizes to knobs on a radio. The distance you could dial depended on the size of the knobs. This girl was well-endowed and one of the boys said, "You can dial Berlin."

The other girls didn't appreciate the attention the boys were giving her. They came up to the boys who were eyeing her, and asked, "If you took away her sweater, what would you have?" Someone replied, "A big crowd."

Later, this same girl came to school wearing a low cut blouse. Several of the boys were staring. Again, the other girls came up and said, "Are you boys getting your eyes full?" One of the boys replied, "With as much as she is showing, she's going to have to go by a second time."

One day, I made the mistake of saying to one of my classmates that he was acting a little queer. This was 50 years ago and the word was just beginning to refer to homosexual men. Since I was unaware of this new meaning of the word, I couldn't understand why he kept punching me in the arm while the teacher was writing on the blackboard. Repeatedly, I told him to stop, but he refused and finally I took a swing at him. He ducked, lost his balance and fell over backwards on the floor and began moaning. The teacher turned just as he fell and it looked like I had hit him in the face. She sent me to the principal's office convinced that I had punched the student. With the possibility of being expelled, I had to bring my father to school and have a meeting. In the car on the way to school, I kept telling him that I was innocent. He finally stopped the car and asked, "If you could have hit him, would you?" "Sure," I replied. He said, "Then you are guilty, so shut up and take your punishment."

We loved practical jokes. There was one young man in our high school who was quite the Romeo. He liked to take different girls to Giraffe Hill, so named because of all the necking that went on up there. He made the mistake of taking out a girl that my friend liked. We crawled under the car, jacked it up and put a rock under the axle. He was too busy steaming up the windows to notice, but when he tried to leave, the wheels spun and the car wouldn't go. He had to walk the girl home and explain why they were so late getting back. When the girl discovered we were responsible for the disastrous date, she wouldn't have anything to do with him. My friend went around school with a dejected look. When someone remarked that he looked love-sick, we answered, "He's sick because nobody loves him."

I was so skinny that my friends had several jokes about me. For example, if I turned sideways I would disappear. Or if I wore a bow tie it would make me look like a pencil with a ribbon on it. And finally, that if I didn't have an Adams apple, I wouldn't have any shape at all. Those were the years everyone had a nickname. Since I was skinny, I was called "Hacksaw." I was lucky; another poor soul somehow acquired the nickname "Fish-head."

In my neighborhood, which was on the wrong side of the tracks, there were some real characters. One old blind lady nicknamed "Spitting Jenny" would go to the local bar, get drunk, spit, and then stand in the middle of the street and scream obscenities at some poor old Scottish man. I never did get the whole story, but one day he committed suicide and left us his parrot along with some money to take care of it.

This parrot had learned from "Spitting Jenny" and he could really cuss. My mother didn't like the parrot's language, particularly on Sundays. So every Sunday she'd cover the parrot's cage and the bird would sleep thinking it was nighttime. One Monday, she saw the minister coming, so she ran over real fast and covered the cage. As the minister came in the parrot said, "This was one hell of a short week."

I liked the parrot. You could tie a string on each leg and when you pulled one, he would say, "Hello." If you pulled the other leg, he would say, "Goodbye." I showed the trick to a classmate. Not too smart, he asked, "What does he say if you pull both strings?" I told him he would probably say, "I'm going to fall on my ass."

After the war ended, it was time to go back east and visit all the relatives. This was an experience in survival. The day before we left, my father said we had to go to bed at 8:00 p.m., since we were going to get up at 2:00 a.m. to beat the heat going through the desert. We lay there with our eyes wide open, since it was the end of June and the sun was still up. By the time we went to sleep, it was time to get up.

We packed the car with a war surplus tent, a second-hand mattress and all our clothing. My mother had made me a shirt out of a silk parachute with one sleeve longer than the other. Now this is a shirt I wouldn't wear to a dog fight, but she reasoned if we got stranded at least I'd have something to wear. The car was so full of clothes, the tent and camping equipment, there wasn't any room left for us. Our legs stuck straight up. We looked like a family of migrant farm workers out of the Grapes of Wrath.

On the front bumper of the car, we hung a water bag. My Dad said we would have cool water to drink when we stopped in the desert. We had cool water all right, but it seemed a lot of bugs gave their lives to make it green. When we got back east, people started yelling, "Hey! You got something dragging on your front bumper."

As it turned out, we really didn't need the water bag. My father was an easy-going man until he got behind the wheel of a car. We quickly learned not to drink a lot of liquids, since it would be at least four hours until the next stop.

My Mom brought a big bottle of peanut butter and a loaf of white bread. After one day of this diet, we didn't even need bathroom breaks. I still believe this was a diabolical plot by my father, since he didn't want to stop for anything except gas. To make life more miserable, cars back then didn't have air conditioning. The conversation in the back wasn't, "Are we there yet?" It was, "Put your arm down."

Forget about motels and restaurants. We stopped at parks where we pitched the tent and spent the night. Of course, my father drove well into the night and one pitch dark night we spotted a green lawn and lots of trees and assumed it was a park. The next morning I rolled over on a stone that said "Rest in Peace." We had spent the night in a cemetery.

We had to live through the depression and several wars. Therefore, some young people don't understand how we think.

A college student at a football game challenged a senior citizen sitting next to him, saying it was impossible for their generation to understand his. "You grew up in a different world," the student said, loud enough for the whole crowd to hear. "Today we have television, jet planes, space travel, man has walked on the moon, our spaceships have visited Mars, and we even have nuclear energy, electric and hydrogen cars, computers with light-speed processing, and..." Taking advantage of a pause in the student's litany, the geezer said, "You're right. We didn't have those things when we were young; so we invented them, you little twit! What are you doing for the next generation?"

The following was on the Internet, author unknown:

How Old Is Grandpa?

One evening, a grandson was talking to his grandfather about current events. The grandson asked his grandfather what he thought about the shootings at schools, the computer age, and just things in general.

The Grandpa replied, "Well, let me think a minute. I was born before television, polio shots, frozen foods, Xerox, contact lenses, Frisbees and the pill. There were no credit cards, laser beams or ball-point pens. Most homes did not have air conditioners, dishwashers or clothes dryers. The clothes were hung out to dry in the fresh air and man had yet to walk on the moon.

Your Grandmother and I got married first and then lived together. Most families had a father and a mother. Until I was 25, I called every woman older than I, "Ma'am," and after I turned 25, I still called policemen and every man with a title, "Sir."

We were before gay-rights, computer-dating, dual careers, day-care centers and group therapy. Our lives were governed by the Ten Commandments, good judgment and common sense. We were taught to know the difference between right and wrong and to stand up and take responsibility for our actions. Serving your country was a privilege; living in this country was a bigger privilege. We thought fast food was what people ate during Lent. Having a meaningful relationship meant getting along with your cousins. Draft dodgers were people who closed their front doors when the evening breeze started.

Time-sharing meant time the family spent together in the evenings and weekends, not purchasing condominiums. We never heard of FM radios, tape decks, CDs, computers, yogurt, or guys wearing earrings. We listened to the Big Bands, Jack Benny and the President's speeches on our radios. And I don't ever remember any kid blowing his brains out listening to Tommy Dorsey. If you saw anything with "Made in Japan" on it, it was junk. The term, "making out," referred to how you did on our school exam. Pizza Hut, McDonald's and instant coffee were unheard of.

We had 5 & 10 cent stores where you could actually buy things for 5 and 10 cents. Ice cream cones, phone calls, rides on a streetcar, and a Pepsi were all a nickel. And if you didn't want to splurge, you could spend your nickel on enough stamps to mail one letter and two post cards.

You could buy a new Chevy Coupe for $1200.00, but who could afford one? Too bad, because gas was 20 cents a gallon.

In my day, "grass" was mowed, "coke" was a cold drink, "pot" was something your mother cooked in, and "rock music" was your grandmother's lullaby. "Aids" were helpers in the Principal's office, "chip" meant a piece of wood, "hardware" was found in a hardware store, and "software" wasn't even a word.

And we were the last generation to actually believe that a lady needed a husband to have a baby. No wonder people call us "old and confused" and they say there is a generation gap. And how old do you think grandpa is. Read on to see—pretty scary if you think about it and pretty sad at the same time. Think how time has changed.

Grandpa is only 54.

Today, why do younger people order double cheeseburgers, large fries, and a Diet Coke? And, why do they leave cars worth thousands of dollars in the driveway and put their useless junk in the garage?

Old age, I decided, isn't all bad. I am now the person I should have always been. Oh, not my body—the wrinkles, baggy eyes and sagging skin. I am distressed by the old person who lives in my mirror, but I don't agonize over those things for long. I would never trade my amazing friends, my wonderful life and my loving family for less gray hair or a flatter belly. I realize some did not make it to this age, so I've become kinder to myself and less critical of others. I am no longer trying to prove anything. I now have to accept my personality flaws for without them I might not have any personality at all.

Do you feel that when you get older that you become a nobody? Just tell them that nobody is perfect; so you must be perfect.

# 10 The Internet

This chapter includes some gems—material, jokes and stories that friends and family found on the Internet and forwarded to me. The authors are unknown. I hope you enjoy them as much as I did.

An unmarried woman noted that old aunts used to come up to her at weddings, poke her in the ribs, and cackle, telling her, "You're next." They stopped after she started doing the same thing at funerals.

If God told Noah to build another ark today, He would find things have changed. He would need a building permit and argue with the inspector about the need for a sprinkler system. The neighbors would claim that he was violating the neighborhood Home Owner's Association laws by building the ark in his yard and exceeding the height limit. Getting the wood would be another problem. There would be a ban on cutting trees in order to save the spotted owl. He would be sued by the animal rights group; they would insist that he was confining wild animals against their will. The EPA would require an environmental impact study on God's proposed flood. The immigration agency would claim he was leaving the country illegally with endangered species and he would be put in jail.

Some old men at a rest home told their jokes so many times, they knew them by heart. They assigned numbers to each joke and when a joke was appropriate to the situation, someone said the number and they all laughed. One day a new arrival decided he would try it. He called out a number and nobody laughed. When he asked why, they told him, "You just don't know how to tell a joke."

An old man and a young boy were traveling village to village selling pots off a small cart pulled by a donkey. The boy rode in the cart and the old man walked. As they went along they passed some people who remarked it was a shame the old man was walking and the boy was riding. The man and boy thought maybe the critics were right, so they changed positions.

Later, they passed some people that remarked, "What a shame, he makes that little boy walk." They decided they both would walk. Soon they passed some more people who thought they were stupid to walk when they had a decent cart to ride. So, they both rode the cart.

Now they passed some people that shamed them by saying, "How awful to make that poor donkey pull such a heavy load." The boy and man said they were probably right, so they decided to put the donkey in the cart and pull it themselves. On a steep mountain road they lost their grip on the cart, and it rolled off a cliff and the donkey was killed. The moral of the story? If you listen to other people on how to run your business, you're going to lose your ass.

An elderly widow was so lonesome living alone that some of her friends talked her into getting a pet as a companion. The pet shop suggested that she purchase a talking parrot that would keep her company.

Upon bringing the parrot home, she found her to be quite a joy—until one day when the widow decided to have some of her friends in for a visit. When the parrot saw some of the guests were men, she fluffed up her wings and said in a loud voice, "Hello boys, I'm Sally the swinger!"

This embarrassed the widow so terribly that she quickly took the parrot to the basement and put a cover over her cage. "What will I do with her?" she wondered. "It would be too embarrassing to take her back to the pet store." Then, she thought, "I know, I'll take her to the church. The priest will know what to do with her."

The priest said, "Don't you worry about her. I have two parrots that are good Catholics. We'll put her in between them and they will teach her some manners." When the priest and the widow left the room, Sally fluffed her wings and said to the priest's parrots, "Hello boys, I'm Sally the swinger!"

One of the priest's parrots looked over to the other one and said, "Put up your rosary, our prayers have been answered!"

Two old town drunks were walking along railroad tracks. One said to the other, "This is the longest set of stairs I have ever climbed." The other one replied, "Yes, it is, but I don't mind the steps as much as I do these short handrails."

SENIOR THOUGHTS:

- Growing older is mandatory; growing up is optional.
- Never take a sleeping pill when you have eaten prunes.
- We have enough youth. How about a fountain of *smart*?
- A turtle only makes progress when it sticks out its neck.
- He who laughs last thinks slowest.
- Seen it all, done it all, can't remember most of it.

- Why is the man who invests all your money called a broker?
- Give a man a fish and he will eat for a day. Teach a man to fish and he will buy an ugly hat and sit in a boat all day drinking beer.
- If the shoe fits, get another one just like it.
- Why should I waste my time reliving the past when I can spend it worrying about the future?
- False hope is better than no hope at all.
- To have a successful relationship, I must learn to make it look like I'm giving as much as I'm getting.
- Why do drugstores make the sick walk all the way to the back of the store to get their prescriptions, while healthy people can buy cigarettes at the front?
- Why it is that doctors call what they do "practice?"
- If you don't learn to laugh at trouble, you won't have anything to laugh at when you're old.
- Why do they lock gas station bathrooms? Are they afraid someone will clean them?
- In some cultures what I do would be considered normal.

An old woman who had lived her whole life in a small town was a witness to a crime. She was called to testify in court. The defense attorney asked if she knew the prosecuting attorney and she replied, "Yes. When he was a little boy he was a conniving, ambitious kid who would do anything to get ahead. Now, he would even put his own mother in jail if it helped his career." The prosecution attorney then asked if she knew the defense attorney. She said, "Yes. When he was a little boy he was always chasing the buck and would do anything to get money, even if he had to lie and cheat. He hasn't changed either." The Judge called both attorneys to the bench and told them, "If either one of you asks her if she remembers me, I will get you for contempt of court."

An old man's little dog died. He had owned the pet for many years. He said, "I don't know what I'll do without him. He's been a companion to me for so long. I know what I'll do. I'll bury him in the backyard and when I miss him, I'll just say, 'he's out in the back yard,' and it will satisfy me. But, I really should make sure he's dead before I bury him. I'll take him to the vet to make sure."

The veterinarian looked at the dog and said, "Yes, he's dead." The man asked, "Can you give me some proof that he is dead?" The vet left the room and came back with a big tomcat and said, "Check him out, Tommy." The cat walked around the dog, sniffing at his eyes, ears, mouth, and feet a couple of times. Then the cat sat at the end of the table and looked up at the vet. The vet said, "There's your proof. The dog is very dead." The man wrapped up the dog again and asked, "How much do I owe you, doctor?" The vet replied, "That will be $250.00." The man was shocked. "What cost so much, doctor?" The doctor replied, "Well, an office visit is a standard $50.00, but I'll have to charge you $200.00 for the 'Cat's Scan!'"

The 98-year-old Mother Superior from Ireland was dying. The nuns gathered around her bed trying to make her last journey comfortable. They gave her some warm milk to drink, but she refused. Then one of the nuns took the glass back to the kitchen. Remembering a bottle of Irish whiskey received as a gift the previous Christmas, she opened and poured a generous amount into the warm milk.

Back at Mother Superior's bed, she held the glass to her lips. Mother Superior drank a little, then a little more and before they knew it, she had drunk the whole glass down to the last drop. "Mother," the nuns asked with earnest, "please give us some wisdom before you die." She raised herself up in bed and with a pious look on her face said, "Don't sell that cow."

An elderly couple went into a fast food restaurant and ordered a hamburger, French fries and a soft drink, asking for an extra cup. The man proceeded to divide the hamburger, count out equal numbers of the fries and pour half the drink in the second cup. A businessman watching this, came over to the table and said, "Excuse me, I can well afford purchasing you another order so you would each have a meal." The lady replied quickly, "Oh, no, this is the way we do everything. We share everything." The businessman went back to his table and watched the man enjoying his meal while his wife sat with her arms folded, watching her husband eat. The businessman couldn't take it any longer. He went back to the table and asked, "Why aren't you eating? You're just sitting there watching your husband enjoy his meal." The lady said again, "Like I said, we share everything alike—I am waiting for the teeth!"

An old, drunk man arrived at JFK Airport and wandered around the terminal with tears streaming down his cheeks. An airline employee asked him if he was already homesick. "No," replied the old man. "I've lost all my luggage!" "How'd that happen?" the employee asked. "The cork fell out!" he cried.

Two nuns sat in a cafe and watched the brothel across the street. They saw a Baptist minister walk into the brothel, and one of them said, "Aye, 'tis a shame to see a man of the cloth going bad." Then they saw a Rabbi enter the brothel, and the other nun said, "Aye, 'tis a shame to see that the Jews are falling victim to temptation." Then they saw a Catholic priest enter the brothel, and one of the Irish nuns said, "What a terrible pity. One of the girls must be quite ill."

Muldoon lived alone in the Irish countryside with only a pet dog for company. One day, the dog died and Muldoon went to the parish priest and said, "Father, my dog is dead. Could ya' be sayin' a mass for the poor creature?" Father Patrick replied, "I'm afraid not. We cannot have services for an animal in the church. But there is a new denomination down the lane, and there's no telling what they believe. Maybe they'll do something for the creature." Muldoon said, "I'll go right away Father. Do ya' think $1,000 is enough to donate for the service?" Father Patrick exclaimed, "Sweet Mary, Mother of Jesus! Why didn't ya' tell me the dog was Catholic?"

An Irish priest was driving down to New York and got stopped for speeding. The state trooper smelled alcohol on the priest's breath. He said, "Sir, have you been drinking?" "Just water," said the priest. The trooper said, "Then why do I smell wine?" The priest said, "Good Lord! He's done it again!"

SINCE I'VE MATURED...

- I've learned that you cannot make someone love you. All you can do is to hang around them and hope they get tired and give in.
- I've learned that one good turn gets most of the blankets.
- I've learned that no matter how much I care, some people are just jackasses.

- I've learned that it takes years to build up trust, and it only takes suspicion, not proof, to destroy it.
- I've learned that whatever hits the fan will not be evenly distributed.
- I've learned that you shouldn't compare yourself to others; they are more screwed up than you think.
- I've learned that depression is merely anger without enthusiasm.
- I've learned that it is not what you wear; it is how you take it off.
- I've learned that ex's are like fungus and keep coming back.
- I've learned that I don't suffer from insanity, I enjoy it.
- I've learned that we are responsible for what we do, unless we are celebrities.
- I've learned that artificial intelligence is not a match for natural stupidity.
- I've learned that the people you care most about in life are taken from you too soon and the less important ones just never go away. The real pains in the ass are permanent.
- I've learned age is a very high price to pay for maturity.

A man was lamenting at the lunch counter that he could not eat anything but "mush" due to having all his teeth pulled. He was waiting to get enough money to buy a set of teeth. The man next to him pulled out a set of teeth and said, "Try these to see if they fit." He handed them back and said, "These are too small." The stranger then reached into another pocket and handed him another pair and said, "These should be a little bigger." They were a perfect fit. The man asked, "Are you a tooth salesman? Are these for sale?" The stranger replied, "No, you can have them. You see, I'm an undertaker."

An old drunk staggered into a Catholic Church and sat down in a pew. The man's tie was stained; his face was plastered with red lipstick, and a half bottle of Bacardi stuck out of his torn coat pocket. He opened his newspaper and began reading.

A priest came over and sat near him, and after a few minutes, the man turned to the priest and asked, "Say, Father, d'ya know what causes arthritis?" "Yes, my son, it's caused by loose living, being with cheap, wicked women, drinking too much alcohol, having contempt for your fellow men, and lack of bathing." "Well, I'll be damned," the drunk muttered, returning to his paper. The priest, thinking about what he had said, nudged the man and apologized, saying: "I'm very sorry. I didn't mean to come on so strongly. How long have you had arthritis?" "I don't have it, Father. I was just reading here that the Pope does."

The old drunk then entered a confessional booth, sat down, but said nothing. The Priest entered the adjacent booth and coughed a few times to get his attention but the drunk just sat there. Finally, the Priest pounded three times on the wall. The drunk mumbled, "Ain't no use knocking, there's no paper on this side either."

An old man had two 50-yard line tickets for the Super Bowl. At the end of the first quarter, the seat next to him was empty. A man came down and asked the old man if anyone was sitting in the seat next to him. "No, " he said, "the seat is empty." "This is incredible," said the man. "Who would have a seat like this for the Super Bowl, the biggest sport event in the world, and not use it?" Somberly, the man says, "Well, the seat actually belongs to me. I was supposed to come here with my wife, but she passed away. This is the first Super Bowl we have not been to together since we got married in 1957." "Oh, I'm so sorry to hear that, that's terrible. But couldn't you find someone else—a friend, relative or even a neighbor to take the seat?" The man shook his head, "No they're all at her funeral."

During one particularly icy winter, an older couple from Minneapolis decided to go to Florida for a long weekend to thaw out. They planned to stay at the very same hotel where they spent their honeymoon 30 years ago. Because both had jobs, they found it difficult coordinating their travel schedules. It was decided that the husband would fly to Florida on a Thursday and his wife would follow him the next day.

Upon arriving as planned, the husband checked into the hotel. In his room, there was a computer, so he decided to send his wife an e-mail back in Minneapolis. However, he accidentally left out one letter in her address, and sent the e-mail without realizing his error. In Houston, a widow had just returned from her husband's funeral. The dearly departed was a minister of many years who had been called home to glory following a heart attack. The widow checked her e-mail, expecting messages from relatives and friends. Upon reading the first message, she fainted. The widow's son rushed into the room, found his mother on the floor, and saw the computer screen which read:

*My Loving Wife*

*Subject: I've arrived.*

*I know you're surprised to hear from me. They have computers here now and you are allowed to send e-mails to your loved ones. I've just arrived and have been checked in. I see that everything has been prepared for your arrival tomorrow. Looking forward to seeing you then. Hope your journey is as uneventful as mine was.*

*P.S. Sure is hot down here.*

A man was telling his neighbor, "I just bought a new hearing aid. It cost me $4,000, but it's state of the art. It's perfect." "Really, what kind is it?" asked the neighbor. "Twelve-thirty."

A woman was leaving a 7-11 with her morning coffee when she noticed a most unusual funeral procession approaching the nearby cemetery. A long black hearse was followed by a second long black hearse about 50 feet behind. Behind the second hearse was a solitary elderly woman walking a pit bull dog on a leash. Behind her were about 200 women walking single file. The woman couldn't stand the curiosity. She respectfully approached the woman walking the dog and said, "I am so sorry for your loss, and I know now is a bad time to disturb you, but I've never seen a procession like this. Whose funeral is it?" The woman replied, "Well, that first hearse is for my husband." "What happened to him?" The woman replied, "My dog attacked and killed him." She inquired further, "I'm sorry. Who is in the second hearse?" "His mistress. She tried to help my husband when the dog turned on her." A poignant and thoughtful moment of silence passed between the two women. "Can I borrow the dog?" she asked. "Get in line," the old woman said.

Three old guys were out walking. First one said, "Windy, isn't it?" Second one said, "No, it's Thursday." Third one said, "So am I. Let's go get a beer."

When the store manager returned from lunch, he noticed his clerk's hand was bandaged, but before he could ask about the bandage, the clerk had some very good news for him. "Guess what, sir?" the clerk said proudly. "I finally sold that terrible, ugly suit we've had so long." "Do you mean that repulsive pink and blue double-breasted thing?" the manager asked. "That's the one," said the clerk. "That's great!" the manager cried. "I thought we'd never get rid of that monstrosity. That had to be the ugliest suit we've ever had. But tell me, why is your hand bandaged?" "Oh," the clerk replied, "after I sold the guy that suit, his seeing-eye dog bit me."

The following was overheard at a recent party: "My ancestry goes back all the way to Alexander the Great," said Christine. She then turned to Miriam and asked, "How far back does your family go?" "I don't know," replied Miriam. "Our records were lost in the flood."

Just got this in from a reliable source: It seems there is a virus called the "Senile Virus" that even the most advanced programs of Norton and McAfee cannot take care of it. So be warned. The virus appears to affect those of us who were born before 1950.

Symptoms of the Senile Virus:

1. Causes you to send the same e-mail twice.
2. Causes you to send blank e-mail.
3. Causes you to send e-mail to the wrong person.
4. Causes you to send e-mail back to the person who sent it to you.
5. Causes you to forget to attach attachments.
6. Causes you to hit "send" before you've finished the e-mail.

Billy was on his deathbed with his wife, Jenny, maintaining a steady vigil by his side. As she held his fragile hand, her warm tears ran silently down her face, splashed onto his face and roused him from his slumber. He looked up and his pale lips began to move slightly. "My darling Jenny," he whispered. "Hush, my love," she said, "Go back to sleep, Shhh, don't talk." But he was insistent. "Jenny," he said in his tired voice, "I have to talk; I have something I must confess to you." "There's nothing to confess," replied the weeping Jenny. "It's all right, everything's all right, go to sleep now." "No, no. I must die in peace, Jenny. I slept with your sister, your best friend and our next door neighbor." Jenny mustered a pained smile and stroked his hand. "Hush now, Billy. Don't torment yourself. I know all about it, that is why I poisoned you."

The following are quotes from Bob Hope regarding aging:

*On turning 70:* "You still chase women, but only downhill."

*On turning 80:* "That's the time of your life when even your birthday suit needs pressing."

*On turning 90:* "You know you're getting old when the candles cost more than the cake."

*On turning 100:* "I don't feel old. In fact, I don't feel anything until noon. Then it's time for my nap."

*On giving up his early career of boxing:* "I ruined my hands in the ring ... the referee kept stepping on them."

*On sailors:* "They spend the first six days of each week sowing their wild oats, then they go to church on Sunday and pray for crop failure."

*On never winning an Oscar:* "Welcome to the Academy Awards or, as it's called at my home, 'Passover'."

*On golf:* "Golf is my profession. Show business is just to pay the green fees."

*On Presidents:* "I have performed for 12 presidents and entertained only six."

God grant me the senility to forget the people I never liked anyway, the good fortune to run into the ones I do and the eyesight to tell the difference. Now that I'm 'older' (but refuse to grow up), here's what I've discovered:

- I started out with nothing, and I still have most of it. My wild oats have turned into prunes and All Bran. I finally got my head together; now my body is falling part. Funny, I don't remember being absent minded.

- All reports are in; life is now officially unfair. If all is not lost, where is it?

- It is easier to get older than it is to get wiser.

- Some days you're the dog; some days you're the hydrant. I wish the buck stopped here; I sure could use a few. Kids in the back seat cause accidents. Accidents in the back seat cause kids.

- It's hard to make a come back when you haven't been anywhere, and the only time the world beats a path to your door is when you're in the bathroom.

- If God wanted me to touch my toes, he would have put them on my knees. When I'm finally holding all the cards, why does everyone decide to play chess?

- It's not hard to meet expenses. They're everywhere. The only difference between a rut and a grave is the depth.

- Always keep your words soft and sweet, just in case you have to eat them.

- Just when I was getting used to yesterday, along came today.

THE DIFFERENCE 30 YEARS MAKES:

| 1975 | 2005 |
|---|---|
| Long hair | Longing for hair |
| KEG | EKG |
| Acid rock | Acid reflux |
| The perfect high | The high yield mutual fund |
| Moving to California- because it's cool. | Moving to California- because it's warm. |
| Growing pot | Growing pot belly |
| Seed and stems | Roughage |
| Killer weed | Weed killer |
| Hoping for BMW | Hoping for a BM |
| The Grateful Dead | Dr. Kevorkian |
| Going to a new Hip joint | Receiving a new hip joint |
| Rolling Stones | Kidney Stones |
| Screw the system | Upgrade the system |
| Disco | Costco |
| Passing the driver's test | Passing the vision test |

While attending a marriage seminar on communication, an old man and his wife listened to the instructor as he declared, "It is essential that husbands and wives know the things that are important to each other." He addressed the men, "Can you describe your wife's favorite flower?" The old man leaned over, touched his wife's arm gently and whispered, "Pillsbury All-Purpose, isn't it?"

AFTER 60 YEARS I STILL DON'T KNOW WHY...

- How important does a person have to be before they are considered assassinated instead of just murdered? If money doesn't grow on trees then why do banks have branches?
- Since bread is square, then why is sandwich meat round? Why do you have to "put your two cents in" but it's only a "penny for your thoughts?" Where's that extra penny going to?
- Why does a round pizza come in a square box? What did cured ham actually have? How is it that we put man on the moon before we figured out it would be a good idea to put wheels on luggage?
- Why is it that people say they "slept like a baby" when babies wake up like every two hours? If a deaf person has to go to court, is it still called a hearing? Why are you *in* a movie, but you're *on* T.V.?

- Why do people pay to go up tall buildings and then put money in binoculars to look at things on the ground?
- How come we choose from just two people for President and 50 for Miss America?
- Why do doctors leave the room while you change? They're going to see you naked anyway.
- Why is "bra" singular and "panties" plural?

I know what Victoria's Secret is. The secret is that nobody older than 30 can fit into their stuff.

There was a man who had worked all of his life and had saved all of his money. He was a real miser when it came to his money. He loved money more than just about anything and just before he died, he said to his wife, "Now listen, when I die, I want you to take all my money and place it in the casket with me. I want to take my money to the afterlife." So he got his wife to promise him with all her heart that when he died, she would put all the money in the casket with him. Well, one day he died. He was stretched out in the casket; the wife was sitting there in black next to her closest friend.

When they finished the ceremony, just before the undertakers got ready to close the casket, the wife said "Wait just a minute!" She had a shoe box with her; she came over with the box and placed it in the casket. Then the undertakers locked the casket down and rolled it away. Her friend said, "I hope you weren't crazy enough to put all that money in the casket." She said, "Yes, I promised. I'm a good Christian, I can't lie. I promised him that I was going to put that money in that casket with him." "You mean to tell me you put every cent of his money in the casket with him?" "I sure did," said the wife. "I got it all together, put it into my account and I wrote him a check."

During the depression, pilots would barnstorm all over the country, and take people for rides in their airplanes for $5.00. At one location an old man came up to the plane and begged his wife to let him take a ride, but she said it cost too much and "Five dollars are five dollars." The same thing happened for the next couple of years and finally the pilot said he would take them both free if she would promise not to make any noise. If she did they would pay the 5 dollars. She agreed, and on the flight the pilot did loops and all kinds of acrobatic maneuvers but not a peep from the back. As he was landing, the pilot said this was the first time he had a woman take the flight and not scream. The old man replied, "Oh, she fell out during the first loop, but like she always said, 'Five dollars are five dollars'."

SENIORS COPING IN THE TWENTY FIRST CENTURY:

1. YOUR reason for not staying in touch with some family and friends is because they do not have e-mail.
2. You have a list of fifteen phone numbers to reach your family of three.
3. You ask your children to send you a JPEG file of their newborn so you can create a screen saver.
4. You pull up in your own driveway and use your cell phone to see if anyone is home.
5. Every commercial on television has a web site address at the bottom of the screen.
6. You buy a computer and three months later it's out of date and sells  for half the price, or less than you paid for it.
7. Leaving the house without your cell phone, which you didn't have the first 40 or 50 years of your life, is now a cause for panic and you turn around to go get it.
8. Using real money, instead of a credit or debit card, to make a purchase would be a hassle and take planning.
9. You just tried to enter your password on the microwave.

10. You consider second-day air delivery painfully slow.

11. Your dining room table is now your flat filing cabinet.

12. Your idea of being organized is multiple-colored Post-it notes.

13. You hear most of your jokes via e-mail instead of in person.

14. You get an extra phone line so you can get phone calls.

15. You disconnect from the Internet and you get this awful feeling, as if you just pulled the plug on a loved one.

16. You get up in the morning and go online before getting your coffee.

17. You wake up at 2 a.m. to go to the bathroom and check your e-mail on your way back to bed.

## AND ALL GOOD STORIES COME TO AN END...

I must end my story because as my family says and threatens to put as an epitaph on my tomb stone, "He finally ran out of gas."

From the Author:

This book was written as the result of an accident. Several months ago, I jumped off my sailboat onto the dock, landed awkwardly and broke my leg. I was in bed for a few weeks until the swelling went down. To combat the boredom, I got out my laptop computer and wrote this book from material that I had been gathering for many years. After the first day I didn't have to take pain pills since I was laughing as I wrote.

On a recent trip to China an older lady of our group hurt her arm and was in severe pain. I shared an original draft of this book with her. She later told me that laughing took her mind off the pain and she felt much better.

A minister's wife wrote that she used a draft also to console a woman whose husband had left her after 20 years of marriage. She said, "I took out your book and we read together for 45 minutes and by then she was laughing so hard, I thought she would fall to the floor. I plan to use your book when any of the members of our church comes to me for comfort."

Another woman wrote. "I started reading it in the waiting room at the doctor's office and sat there and laughed, chuckled and probably drove the others waiting nuts. This is so cute. John Hacker has such a sense of humor. I showed it to the Doctor and he said he needed one."

It seems this book may be a good therapeutic treatment for pain and depression. I hope you enjoy reading it as much as I enjoyed writing it.

# ORDER FORM

Order additional copies of *Laughing at Growing Old* for loved ones, friends, and colleagues.

**Call 760-340-4517 to order by credit card.**

**Or copy and mail this form and check payable to:**
**I-Form Ink Publishing, Inc., 41-921 Beacon Hill, Suite A,**
**Palm Desert, CA 92211**.

Name: _____

Address: _____

City, State, Zip: _____

_____copies of *Laughing at Growing Old* at $9.95 each _____

    Shipping $2.00 for first book, $1.00 each additional _____
    (No charge for shipping for 6 or more copies)
          California Residents add $.77 tax per book _____

                              Total _____

Payment: _____Check _____MasterCard or Visa

Card #_____

Exp. Date_____ Signature_____

Allow 15 days for delivery. Books can also be ordered on Amazon.com.